UNITED GERMANY
and the
UNITED STATES

Michael A. Freney and Rebecca S. Hartley

NPA Committee on Changing International Realities

NATIONAL PLANNING ASSOCIATION

United Germany and the United States

CIR Report #21
NPA Report #250

Price $17.50

ISBN 0-89068-107-4
Library of Congress
Catalog Card Number 91-60520

Printed in the United States of America

 C439

To
Shelley and Paul

Contents

UNITED GERMANY AND THE UNITED STATES
by Michael A. Freney and Rebecca S. Hartley

MAPS

CHARTS

TABLES

Acknowledgments

The authors are grateful to a wide variety of business and labor leaders, political officials and scholars for their help in dealing with a vital international relationship. It is impossible to list all of these individuals here, but we would like to mention at least some.

Foremost among those who provided guidance for us are the Chair and members of the Board of Advisors for the National Planning Association's Germany Project (listed below) and the members of NPA's Committee on Changing International Realities (listed on pp. 175-177), who offered substantive comments and financial support, provided extensive connections in Germany and in the United States, and helped rid the final product of errors of fact or interpretation. We are indebted to them.

Board of Advisors:
United Germany and the United States

Chair: ROLF HENEL
President, Lederle International,
American Cyanamid Company

C. MICHAEL AHO
Director of Economic Studies and the
International Trade Project,
Council on Foreign Relations, Inc.

EDWARD J. CARLOUGH
General President,
Sheet Metal Workers'
International Association;
Vice Chair, Committee on
Changing International Realities

STEPHEN A. FALK
Managing Director,
Central Europe,
AT&T Deutschland GmbH

ARTHUR M. LERNER
Vice President,
Corporate Development,
Siemens Corporation

JOHN R. MALLOY
Senior Vice President
of External Affairs,
E.I. DuPont de Nemours &
Company

PHILIP D. SHERMAN
Senior Vice President,
Investment Bank Sector,
Citicorp, N.A.

JOHN J. SIMONE
Group Executive,
Manufacturers Hanover
Trust Company;
Chair, Committee on
Changing International Realities

WINFRIED H. SPAEH
Senior General Manager &
Chief Executive USA,
Dresdner Bank AG

HANS G. STORR
Senior Vice President and CFO,
Philip Morris
Companies, Inc.

William R. Miller (former Vice Chairman of the Board of Bristol-Myers Squibb and Chair of the Committee on Changing International Realities at the time this project was conceived) and John J. Simone (Group Executive, Manufacturers Hanover Trust Company and present Chair of the CIR) were especially gracious and helpful. Their counsel to the National Planning Association, and to both of us, has been most beneficial.

We could not have written this book on the basis of research in Washington alone. We are grateful to the corporations listed below that generously provided funds for travel to Europe and in the United States, as well as for publication and dissemination of the study.

SPONSORS: American Cyanamid Company, Bristol-Myers Squibb Company, Schering-Plough Corporation, and Wyeth-Ayerst International

CONTRIBUTORS: G.D. Searle, Johnson & Johnson, Lederle International, Pfizer International, and Warner Lambert Company

Key individuals at three German foundations provided special practical assistance as well as insight and analytical balance. Those foundations are the Konrad-Adenauer-Stiftung, the Friedrich-Ebert-Stiftung and the Friedrich-Naumann-Stiftung. Individual scholars and analysts at the Washington offices of these foundations as well as in Germany tolerated a steady stream of inquiries and responded consistently with helpful good humor.

We are especially grateful to our American and German friends who helped us. We both look forward to the opportunity to reciprocate their many kindnesses.

Michael Brown was instrumental in bringing the two authors together. Special thanks go to Bradley Hecht, NPA Research Assistant, who provided data on which a number of our arguments are based.

Ambassador Edward Masters, President of the National Planning Association, and Dr. Richard Belous, NPA Vice President of International Affairs, endorsed this project at its outset and supported it enthusiastically through its conclusion. Their patience and counsel were major factors in allowing the authors to come to grips with extremely complex and fast-changing developments in U.S.-German relations.

It is important to note that no portion of this work should be taken as or construed to be an official opinion of any government agency. The authors listened carefully to a variety of people, lay and expert, but produced their own analyses. The authors alone are responsible for any remaining errors of fact or interpretation.

On Sources

Almost all of the analysis presented here proceeds from interviews and primary written sources. Experts interviewed were promised anonymity. Primary sources are identified, and key documents are appended.

Certain publications used as background deserve special mention. Among the most useful were two German series available in English. They are:

> *The Week in Germany*
> German Press and Information Service
> The German Information Center
> 950 Third Avenue
> New York, N.Y. 10022

> *The Monthly Report of the Deutsche Bundesbank*
> Deutsche Bundesbank, Frankfurt am Main
> Wilhelm-Epstein-Strasse 14
> P.O.B. 10 06 02
> D-6000 Frankfurt am Main 1

Three British sources were especially valuable. They are:

The *Economist,* the weekly news magazine;

The *Financial Times,* a newspaper published six times weekly;

International Institute for Strategic Studies publications, which include the monthly *Survival,* the occasional *Adelphi Papers* and the annual *Military Balance.*

> International Institute for Strategic Studies
> 23 Tavistock Street
> London WC2E 7NQ
> England

A variety of journals and daily newspapers in the United States and in Germany were consistently helpful, especially given the remarkable pace of events. They are too numerous to cite.

Various publications of the German foundations mentioned in the "Acknowledgments" are essential to scholars trying to keep pace with events in Germany. Information about the foundations' activities and publications is available from their Washington offices:

The Konrad-Adenauer-Stiftung
1330 New Hampshire Avenue, N.W., Suite 104
Washington, D.C. 20036

The Friedrich-Ebert-Stiftung
806 15th Street, N.W., Suite 230
Washington, D.C. 20005

The Friedrich-Naumann-Stiftung
1759 R Street, N.W.
Washington, D.C. 20009

Michael Calingaert's updated study *The 1992 Challenge from Europe: Development of the European Community's Internal Market* (Washington, D.C.: National Planning Association, 1988, with a 1990 Foreword by the author) is an analytical predecessor and useful companion to *United Germany and the United States.*

About the Authors

Michael A. Freney is a private consultant specializing in European political and economic affairs and Director of the Germany Project, part of the program of NPA's Committee on Changing International Realities. He was formerly Senior Fellow and Deputy Chief Operating Officer at the Center for Strategic and International Studies in Washington, D.C. He has also served as Professor of Political Science at the Air Force Academy. Dr. Freney has received degrees from the U.S. Naval Academy, Boston University and Rice University.

Rebecca S. Hartley is a Senior Fellow in the International Program at the National Planning Association and Director of the Germany Project. Ms. Hartley completed undergraduate work at Dartmouth College and received a Master's degree from the University of Virginia, where she is pursuing Ph.D. and J.D. degrees.

Preface

Developments in Germany have riveted the attention of all nations concerned with stability and prosperity in Europe. Many observers anticipated change in the post-World War II environment, but few believed that the pace of change would be so swift. Few were sanguine about the potential for a smooth transition between the so-called Cold War environment and whatever the future holds.

Optimists hope that a combination of market forces and reduced tensions can produce a Europe free of the ideological confrontation that has created conflict and dominated international affairs since World War I. This highly desirable result is clearly not guaranteed.

Uncertainty about the future of the Soviet Union, economic competition, resurgence of nationalism, ethnic tensions, and fear of Germany among its neighbors may all complicate the achievement of a widely shared goal—namely, long-term stability and prosperity in Europe. The "stability" of the Cold War may, in retrospect, look rather attractive to some as the difficulties of transition become more evident.

Although German political, economic and security developments will continue to be primary concerns in terms of the future of Europe, those concerns should not obscure the important role of the United States as an essential player in European affairs. Cultural ties, currency mechanisms, trade pat-

terns, and positions of relative influence make bilateral relations between Germany and the United States an essential element in Europe's developing cohesion and in its progress toward
sustained stability and prosperity.

Informed dialogue between American and German leaders
in business, industry, labor, and government is essential. The
focus of that dialogue should be on opportunities to reconcile
goals and anticipate obstacles to productive, cooperative policy
implementation. The analysis that follows is intended to further
progress in that direction.

The need for such dialogue has long been recognized. The
Marshall Plan would not have succeeded had there not been
good communication between leading Germans and officials in
Washington. Effective diplomatic interaction guided German
economic reconstruction and allowed the commodious accep-
tance of German military participation in the North Atlantic
Treaty Organization. These strong historical precedents suggest
the desirability, if not the necessity, for continued, clear U.S.-
German communication as a key element in the future of
Europe.

However, in the late 1980s, many in Bonn and Washington
became concerned that the quality of dialogue on economic and
security issues was eroding. Policy disagreements over the neutron bomb, the Reykjavik discussions between the United States
and the Soviet Union on nuclear weapons, the growing importance of Germany as a principal player in the European
Community, and the Kohl-Genscher disposition to bargain
directly with Moscow over German and European security created an environment that could easily have led to sharp friction
between Germany and the United States. The atmosphere
became even more electric because of the behavior of the U.S.
Congress, especially liberal elements of the Democratic Party,
regarding the sustained U.S. troop presence in Germany.

The significance of these and other issues led the authors of
this study to propose a comprehensive examination of the future
of the bilateral relationships—political, economic and military—
between Germany and the United States. That proposal, presented to the National Planning Association in August 1989,
was approved on November 2, 1989, seven days before the
Berlin Wall fell. The concerns raised in the original proposal,
however, did not fall with the wall. Germany's changed status
as a European and world power propelled the authors to pursue

even more vigorously their analysis of the importance of informed communication between German and American leaders in government as well as in the private sector.

An important goal of the analysis is to consolidate information for public and private sector leaders dealing with the transition taking place in Europe. A broad range of issues is covered, with emphasis on developments within Germany, the rapidly shifting European economic landscape, and dramatic changes in security arrangements on that continent.

Thorough consideration of the connections among economic welfare, political viability, stability, and prosperity is a *sine qua non* for effective policymaking. In a period of turmoil, that sort of thinking is extremely difficult. Because no single short work can pull together all of the important factors that decisionmakers need to consider, this volume is intended as an overview and a means of helping to single out areas in U.S.-German relations where cooperation or conflict is most likely.

CHAPTER ONE

Unification in Perspective

Preoccupation with the events associated with German unification may obscure fundamental and prerequisite changes that occurred in Europe before public discussion of near-term German unification even began. To be sure, dramatic occurrences such as the fall of the Berlin Wall on November 9, 1989, the first free election in the east German *Laender* (states) in 57 years on March 18, 1990, and the formal vote to unify on October 3, 1990, were important milestones. Perhaps the most significant of these was the agreement among the victorious allies of World War II and the two Germanies that unification should proceed (see Appendix 6). However, unification itself is best viewed as a process rather than as an event. Although those events in 1989 and 1990 are fascinating to people concerned with the future shape of European civilization, the redrawing of Germany's political structure is only one of the fundamental changes to take into account. That the political, economic and security boundaries of all of Europe have shifted must also be considered. Indeed, true unification involves political, economic and security adjustments that will take money, time and effort. How much money and time and by whose efforts are key questions that will remain only partially answered in the near term.

The most important prerequisite for the recent changes in Europe has been the veritable collapse of both communist ideology and Soviet influence. Mikhail Gorbachev's abandonment of traditional Marxism-Leninism and his accompanying decision to abandon the hegemonic aspirations of the Soviet Union in Europe are major and welcome developments. But continuation of existing trends is by no means guaranteed. Further, change in Soviet behavior, while a necessary underlying condition for the largely peaceful revolutions of 1989-90, does not alone ensure successful transitions to democracy and capitalism in eastern Europe.

Germany leads the transition from command to market economies that is occurring within east European countries. Attention is thus bound to center on Germany's progress, and the policies and programs it adopts will affect those adopted elsewhere, although those nations will be unable to pursue eastern Germany's exact policies and programs. As the financial and social costs of eastern Germany's transition to a market economy become clearer, politicians and officials concerned with rebuilding the rest of central and eastern Europe will be trying to learn from the German experience.

GERMANY'S PIVOTAL POSITION

A unified Germany is far greater in importance and potential than the sum of the Federal Republic of Germany (FRG) and the German Democratic Republic (GDR). The German state is centrally located in Europe and is the most important in terms of population and area (see Table 1.1). Differences between east and west notwithstanding, the capacity of the unified German economy to expand is unquestioned. Germany's

TABLE 1.1
Germany's Size and Population

	Population (1990)	Area
United Germany	78,500,000	357,050 km^2
FRG	61,700,000	248,713 km^2
GDR	16,800,000	108,337 km^2

TABLE 1.2
West and East German GDP, 1989
(Billion)

West Germany	DM	2,260
East Germany	OM	280-350

Sources: Deutsche Bundesbank and *The Economist.*

record as an exporter is remarkable. The current account surplus of the Federal Republic alone in 1989 was approximately DM 100 billion. Even the difficulties involved in raising the standard of productivity in eastern Germany to that in western Germany seem manageable in light of the west's track record.

The gross domestic product (GDP) of the two Germanies only partially reflects the productive capacity likely to emerge as the fetters of communism are removed in the east (see Table 1.2). The German people are highly educated, productive and disciplined. A substantial labor pool combining east and west German talent is one of the strongest assets of the newly unified nation (Table 1.3). The labor force in eastern Germany will undoubtedly add to the substantial capacity of the west to export finished products such as ground and aerospace vehicles, machines and electrical products, iron and steel, computers, optics, and other high technology products.

TABLE 1.3
Employment by Sector, 1988
(Percent of Total)

	Eastern Germany	**Western Germany**
Agriculture	11	5
Manufacturing	49	39
Services	24	37
Trade and transport	17	19

Sources: Institut der Deutschen Wirtschaft (Cologne), Deutsche Bundesbank and German government sources.

COSTS OF UNIFICATION

Many practical difficulties associated with unification induce resentment among both east and west Germans. Most of that resentment currently centers on the costs to individual Germans of implementing unification and on the requirements that east Germans radically modify their social support structure and work ethic. Many in western Germany believe that the immense and still incalculable financial costs of integrating the eastern states will result in higher taxes and slower economic growth for the new, broader German economy.

Estimates of costs vary widely and tend to reflect the political agendas of those doing the calculations. Difficulties associated with estimating the practical costs of modernization are dramatic. For example, it makes a difference in estimations if a telecommunications system is being upgraded to meet present standards or to set a new standard for the 21st century. Further, the cost of maintaining adequate social welfare systems in the eastern states will vary according to one's definition of "adequate." The cost of cleaning up environmentally toxic sites cannot accurately be estimated when the extent and even the location of pollution damage are often widely undocumented. Concerned parties find it difficult to agree on anything but tentative order-of-magnitude price tags.

Likewise, an outside observer's personal perspectives on political realities in Germany influence, in some measure, whether that individual should believe a particular estimate at a particular time. However, one reality seems clear: current estimates have already changed and will continue to change as political priorities, imperatives and influence change within Germany's federal structure. Not only do estimates potentially reflect personal and political agendas, but they are also highly suspect because of the lack of western-style accounting data for, and practices in, east German enterprises.

Determination of the likely division of the financial costs of unification among the German government, private industry and capital markets significantly depends on accurate estimates of costs. Decisions on apportionment necessarily reflect any biases of the cost estimates upon which they are based.

A UNIFIED GERMANY IN EUROPE

Some foreign analysts fear that preoccupation with unification will constrain Germany's ability to act decisively and influentially in international affairs. Certainly, in the near term, such constraints will operate in some areas. Germans will pay whatever amounts are necessary to guarantee the stability of their eastern states. This is likely to lead to substantial short-term change in German influence on international capital markets and especially in the German current account balance. But extensive attention to the near term may lead observers to give short shrift to the more important medium- and long-term effects of the conditions that enabled unification to become a reality. (For Germany after unification, see Map 1, p. 6.)

Still other analysts believe that unification portends the development of an economic superpower in Europe that will wield enormous sway over its neighbors. Proponents of this view dismiss the arithmetic total of "east plus west Germany" as being a misleadingly low indicator of German economic influence. Instead, they postulate a second economic miracle for Germany that will lead to substantially more economic power than the mere addition of east and west would indicate. The development of such a colossus within the European Community, they argue, will significantly amplify the relative strength of Germany. There is no gainsaying this point. Not only is Germany larger, not only will it play a much more powerful role in the EC, but unified Germany, for better or for worse, is the pivotal player in the center of all Europe (see Map 2, p. 7).

Germany's achievement of national sovereignty means that its western partners should be prepared for greater German initiative and self-confidence. Helmut Kohl's unilateral announcement of his November 1989 "10 point plan" and his bilateral negotiations with Gorbachev are reflections of new German confidence and assertiveness in international affairs rather than exceptions to Germany's somewhat self-effacing postwar *modus operandi*. Similarly, German history will continue to affect the way in which united Germany's international and domestic actions will be perceived by its western and eastern neighbors and partners. A period of nervous adjustment in attitude among Germany's neighbors is likely as German confidence and influence grow.

MAP 1
Germany After Unification

Note: Germany is composed of 16 States. The total area is 357,000 square kilometers, and the population is 78.5 million.

MAP 2
Europe

The increase in Germany's power in Europe has not occurred simply because of unification. Rather, it is a result of a condition that permitted unification to occur at all—the collapse of Soviet power. The problem of developing a stable central Europe was only postponed, not solved, by Soviet hegemony there. Looking back, it was arguably Germany's inability to balance such a role within Europe that contributed to two world wars in this century.

Germany in the 1990s and beyond must look both east and west as it pursues its policy goals. The Chancellor, and even his opponents, continually express the German commitment to western values and to the various international arrangements that have led to peace and prosperity in western Europe. Simultaneously, as noted above, Germany will be a role model for east European states struggling toward democracy and market economies. The differences between east and west will not disappear quickly. Germany is likely to experience acutely the tensions these differences generate. Its position as a political and economic leader for all Europe will undoubtedly prove challenging and at times uncomfortable.

That Germany must emerge at the same time as a world power is a significant complication. There will be serious strains on German economic and political resources as Germany fits itself to its new positions. Not the least of German concerns will be maintaining cordial relations with its existing partners, especially the United States.

GERMAN POWER AND AMERICAN QUESTIONS

Potential for tension exists in the economic and security dimensions of U.S.-German relations. Nevertheless, a tradition of cooperation and goodwill has emerged in U.S.-German relations from the time of the Marshall Plan to the present. Can that tradition be preserved as Germany acquires new power and influence in the world at large? Where do the principal opportunities for cooperation or disagreement lie?

Germany, by itself and in its role as the leader of the European Community, is of vital importance to America's economic and military security. Sensitivity in Washington to the volatile conditions surrounding unified Germany is essential if enlightened U.S. policy initiatives are to prosper and serve both nations well.

One does not have to be a doomsayer to note that although the United States remains the strongest economy in the world, relative American political and economic influence in western Europe has declined over the past decades. As western Europe has become more self-reliant and more prosperous, most of its nations have gained relatively in economic and political flexibility.

This is not to say that American power has declined in absolute terms. Rather, the international leverage of other nations has grown, often it seems, at the expense of U.S. leadership. For example, the deutsche mark has replaced the U.S. dollar as a reserve and trading currency in many areas, and it is the currency of reference in Europe. The U.S. share of world trade and investment has declined. American military leadership was called into question in Europe during and after the Vietnam War. President Ronald Reagan's unilateral military pronouncements were often resented by Europeans, not only because of their content, but also because they often reflected the assumption that the North Atlantic Treaty Organization (NATO) allies would necessarily follow the U.S. lead.

During the 1980s, NATO managed to maintain a generally united front on many important issues. But as the Soviet threat seemed to diminish, so did America's ability to unify other NATO members behind U.S. policy initiatives. The importance of the United States as a counterbalance to the Soviet Union now seems less important to many Europeans as the level of Soviet readiness and the likelihood of a Soviet-initiated conflict in Europe decline.

Perhaps as important for U.S. policymakers to consider, the capacity to avoid public divisions of opinion on policy within NATO has lessened. This has already led and will continue to lead to European questions about American military proposals for European and broader defense programs and to more European proposals for European defense organizations. Disagreements over use of NATO forces outside Europe will not end easily or rapidly in spite of the outcome of the war in the Persian Gulf.

As the popular perception of the importance of maintaining NATO solidarity declines, other issues are replacing military ones as most salient in the eyes of western policymakers and publics. Economic issues associated with defense are gaining public visibility.

The decline in importance of military force as a factor in European affairs may be temporary or even illusory. Social and economic conflicts persist. In the Soviet Union as well as in the Persian Gulf, the fragility of political and economic systems is apparent. Soviet insistence on dominating the Baltic republics and the naked aggression of Saddam Hussein precipitated situations that serve as stark reminders to those who would wish away fundamental differences of the sort that the Cold War tended to crystallize. The future keeps its own counsel, but no serious student of human affairs, no serious policymaker, no serious business or labor leader can ignore difficulties that cause nations to resort to force.

Although the United States is widely perceived to have performed brilliantly as a military superpower in the Persian Gulf, the opposite is becoming the perception with respect to its domestic economic management. The sorry state of the U.S. financial system in general, the savings and loan crisis, an often dysfunctional public education system, and persistent trade, current account and federal budget deficits as well as comparatively high inflation rates all combine to lead many in Europe to question the value of U.S. leadership in economic fora.

Most Germans consider the FRG to have managed its economic house in an exemplary manner. The Federal Republic has been an almost undisputed economic success. Many Germans believe there are few, if any, countries that can teach Germany anything about economic management. It follows that many Germans believe they should have a substantially higher degree of influence on other countries in international economic discussions and should not need to listen too carefully to U.S. advice. Such sentiments may well create friction between the two nations as economic issues gain prominence and Germany gains confidence in its ability to play a greater international political role.

Many Germans regard the American executive branch as cumbersome at best. U.S. Presidents are looked to for authoritative statements on superpower relations, on European developments and on the importance of democracy as the leading trend in world politics. At that level of generality, Europeans are generally comfortable.

However, when Presidents stake their personal prestige on specific policy decisions like the neutron bomb or "Star Wars," Germans tend to become nervous. Their anxiety is not relieved when they recall occasions when Secretaries of State and Defense have not only disagreed with each other, but also articulated policies somewhat distant from presidential pronouncements.

The U.S. Congress remains largely an enigma to German voters and a tribulation to German policymakers who must consider U.S. perspectives on European developments. The capacity of members of Congress to sally forth with opinions vetted neither in the U.S. executive branch nor among American voters is a legendary source of irritation in European parliamentary democracies. Solace is taken in Germany when congressional leaders of long experience from both sides of the aisle in both Houses solicit European opinions on European matters.

For their part, the Germans have, as one congressional aide put it, "a large stockpile of goodwill" both on Capitol Hill and in the executive branch. That reservoir, however, has the potential to flow away. For example, the substantial cash relief Germany granted to the USSR in fall 1990 came at exactly the time U.S. negotiators were petitioning unsuccessfully for increased German cash and troop commitments for the Persian Gulf effort.

One danger in such situations is that U.S. observers may believe happenstance to be actively anti-American behavior. If divergences of policy goals and conflicts during policy implementation grow, irritation and misunderstandings could further taint relations. Such difficulties are likely to arise in the private sector as well. U.S. executives who have frequent and close contacts with German counterparts sometimes remark on the often substantial political and cultural differences between Germans and Americans. These differences threaten to become more visible if German public and private rhetoric becomes more direct.

Policy consequences of impaired communication may become increasingly significant as Europeans in general, and Germans in particular, recognize that a more unified Europe possesses policy leverage that individual European nations formerly did not have. A more assertive Europe and American sensitivity to erosion of the U.S. position as the clear leader of all democratic states are realities that it is hoped will be taken into account in future relations between Bonn/Berlin and Washington.

In the United States, Chancellor Kohl is regarded as a successful pragmatist. He has consistently satisfied his supporters and confounded his detractors with positions on both foreign and domestic issues that have stood scrutiny in an atmosphere of rapid change. Kohl's leadership in constitutional matters and with regard to currency exchange and his flexibility on the Polish border question have gained him substantial admiration.

German preoccupation with domestic aspects of unification is likely to continue for several years. Germany's effort to equalize standards of living between its west and its east is an undertaking unprecedented in modern history. Success in that effort is essential to stability, not only in Germany, but in Europe as a whole.

The financial and human costs of unification being absorbed by Germans ultimately will benefit all industrialized nations and should benefit Germany's less developed neighbors as well. Patience and tolerance will be necessary among Germany's allies, friends and erstwhile enemies as German government leaders and business executives experiment within new borders and with new sovereign powers and responsibilities.

Communication, cooperation and collaboration can and should be leitmotifs as the turn of the century approaches. Political, economic, social, and military security in today's world are global as well as national goals. But goals are not policies; and policymaking is not implementation.

As ideological constructs cease to dominate debate and economic factors become more salient, a previously bipolar world now is becoming tripolar. The United States, the European Community led by Germany, and Japan are the dominant entities that will determine quality of life in the industrialized world unless military force is introduced by frustrated remnants of totalitarian regimes.

Bilateral relations between the United States and Germany will be an important element in ensuring cooperation between two of the productive giants in the next century. Although sustained and cordial bilateral relations are no substitute for multilateral moves toward peace and stability, American-German cooperation is an underpinning not only for relations among industrialized countries, but also for new openings between north and south.

Europeans in general and Germans in particular frequently accuse the United States of failing to be consistent in its approach to foreign affairs. In a period when Germany will tend to be preoccupied with domestic and regional policies, continued U.S. encouragement of and consideration for German positions and sensitivities are highly desirable. It would be a mistake, however, for German leaders to expect continued fascination with German developments in Washington.

The substantial reservoir of goodwill that exists between Germans and Americans is deep and important. Still, intensive cultivation of understanding through diplomatic, business, educational, and cultural channels is key to the future of the relationship between unified Germany and the United States.

The assumption that continued bilateral cooperation between the United States and Germany is a necessary condition for international stability and prosperity is the basis for subsequent analysis and discussion. That basic assumption can easily lead to the articulation of many different policy objectives. The challenge is to build bridges between those objectives and current realities.

Building such bridges requires the commitment of substantial human and capital resources. But those resources will be ill-used if there is not sufficient effort to refine the broad policy objectives they are meant to fulfill. Redefining objectives must necessarily be a national task. Among friendly powers, that process of redefinition should anticipate obstacles and facilitate cooperation. As the new Europe evolves, U.S.-German bilateral communication can be extremely useful in avoiding misunderstandings in all dimensions of U.S.-European relations and can help the United States continue as a positive influence in European affairs.

Germany's friends, especially the United States, need to be sensitive to German domestic concerns and, indeed, to the strong possibility that those concerns may preoccupy German leaders. Simultaneously, as Germany adjusts to its emergence from four-power oversight, its influence in international affairs is bound to increase. Germany's friends, who have become accustomed to scrupulous German tact in international dealings, may find the Germans less patient and more aggressive. Neither development needs to be regarded as a signal that basic German values have changed.

With the preceding general observations in mind, it is worth noting that there is little certainty about how U.S.-German relationships will evolve. Perhaps the only certainty is that they will evolve. There is little question, however, that evolutions in the form, extent and quality of U.S.-German relations will be conditioned by and take place in the context of three principal issue areas. First is Germany's capacity to proceed successfully in the process of political, economic and social unification. Second is the role that Germany develops for itself within a uniting European economy and in the broader world economy. In those contexts, U.S.-German economic relations will be a key factor. Third, Germany is at a crucial juncture in terms of its position as emerging guarantor of military stability in Europe.

These three topics are key to understanding U.S.-German relations. Internal German factors, economic developments and the changing security environment will be separated initially for analytical reasons, even though the interconnections are more important than the distinctions. The final chapter will be devoted to examining specific policy issues that connect the three areas and that may shape U.S.-German relations as the century draws to an end.

CHAPTER TWO

Uniting Germany

In October 1989, a leading German editor and analyst observed publicly and with emphasis that German unification was unlikely to occur in the 20th century. He may well have been correct. While the legal formalities of unification occurred more rapidly than he anticipated, the social and political end state of the unification process is not yet clearly in view.

Major challenges to successful implementation of the decision to unify are neither few nor always easy to perceive. Some exist primarily within Germany. Others seriously affect the likely course of political, economic and security developments in the European region and beyond.

Key factors within Germany affecting progress toward unification need careful enumeration. Taken together, these factors will condition the outlook of German leaders in terms of domestic politics as well as their approach to international relations, especially with respect to economic and security arrangements evolving in the 1990s.

The basic enumeration here is not intended to be exhaustive. It is problem- and policy-oriented and designed to portray the kaleidoscopic character of change under way in Germany. Subsequent discussion will emphasize the interconnections between Germany and its neighbors. International economic and political factors will be the focus of that analysis.

LEGAL STEPS TOWARD UNIFICATION

The Constitution (Basic Law) of the Federal Republic of Germany, adopted in 1949, specifically foresaw the possibility that Germany would reunite. Under Chancellor Konrad Adenauer's influence, the FRG emerged in the 1950s struggling with the dilemma of how to stay in the west while keeping alive the possibility of ending the postwar partition.

> *"The only road to German unification is European integration, unless we are prepared to renounce freedom."*
>
> Chancellor Konrad Adenauer,
> October 1953

Article 23 of the Basic Law specifies that any German state could use its existing electoral practices to opt for inclusion under the Constitution. That provision became the vehicle for incorporation of the GDR. The combination of a firmly anti-communist showing in the March 18, 1990, east German elections and subsequent decisions among the victorious allies of World War II, the "four powers," led to the Volkskammer decision to accede to the Federal Republic of Germany under article 23. Parallel to this process, the five historical states of the GDR were reconstituted and held their first election as federal states on October 14, 1990. These elections led in turn to the December 2, 1990, all-German election.

Throughout the period between the fall of the Berlin Wall and the all-German election, both east and west Germans showed great sensitivity to legal and political realities. In almost all instances, however, it was the political realities that drove and the legal realities that constrained, albeit slightly, the rush toward formal unification. The principal political driver in the German electoral process was apparent confidence in east and west that Chancellor Kohl and his government could spread prosperity while regaining sovereignty for Germany.

Border questions created some difficulties. Kohl's initial insistence on legal niceties with respect to the western Polish border created anxieties about German irredentist claims. But Kohl and Foreign Minister Hans Dietrich Genscher managed to navigate skillfully through a number of objections to their legalistic position that were raised in Poland, in the Soviet Union and in the west. The result was to acknowledge borders that existed in 1989 between east Germany and Poland, between east Germany and Czechoslovakia, and between west Germany and its various neighbors as the proper confines of a united German state. The four powers formally ratified that decision, essentially re-establishing sovereignty in a fashion that no German government had enjoyed since 1945.

GERMAN ELECTIONS

Three key elections between the fall of the Berlin Wall in November 1989 and the end of 1990 shed light on the outlook in various parts of the new Germany. The east German election on March 18, 1990, produced results that apparently surprised almost everyone. The Christian Democratic Union/Christian Social Union (CDU/CSU) affiliates' 48.2 percent of the vote and the Social Democratic Party (SPD) affiliates' 21.8 percent represented an almost exact reversal of the levels of support for the conservatives and socialists, respectively, anticipated by many political analysts in Germany. East Germans seemed to credit Kohl and Genscher for west German well-being and political initiative far more than they credited Helmut Schmidt and Willy Brandt.

Chart 2.1 shows the results of the October 14, 1990, state elections in the east. This election effectively confirmed the formal decision of October 3 to merge the east German states into the structure established in the Basic Law.

The December 2 all-German election reinforced the notion that prosperity was the voters' principal motivator. The coalition of Kohl's Christian Democrats, the Christian Socialists and Genscher's Free Democrats was strengthened, suggesting that the majority of the German population wished to convey a mandate to the existing leadership to continue leading the unification process (see Table 2.1).

Aside from the electoral process, steps toward unification involved uncertainties and risks that have yet to be fully comprehended. Some of these preceded the official act of unification itself. The most dramatic was currency adjustment.

CURRENCY ADJUSTMENT

A common currency rather than a revised exchange rate turned out to be a necessary political condition for building east Germans' confidence in their future economic development.

CHART 2.1
October 14, 1990, Elections in Five East German States

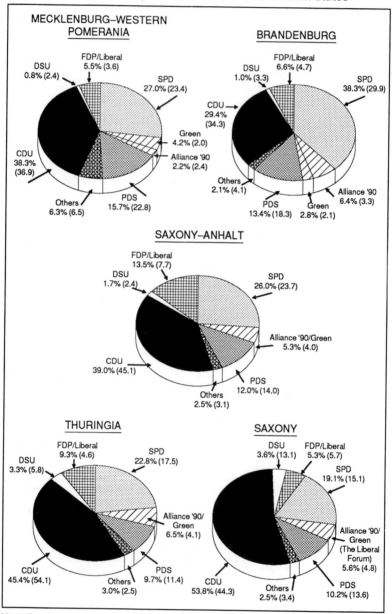

Note: Results in parentheses are from the March 18, 1990 Volkskammer elections.

Sources: *The Week in Germany* and the *Frankfurter Allgemeine Zeitung.*

TABLE 2.1
December 2, 1990, German Elections

Party Name	Number of Votes	Percentage Rate[a]	Seats Awarded
Christian Democratic Party (CDU)	17,051,128	36.7	262
Social Democratic Party (SPD)	15,539,977	33.5	239
Free Democratic Party (FDP)	5,123,936	11.0	79
Christian Social Union (CSU)	3,301,239	7.1	51
Party of Democratic Socialism (PDS) (east)	1,129,290	2.4[b]	17
Alliance '90 (east)	558,552	1.2[b]	8
Green Party (west)	1,788,214	3.9[b]	—
Republicans	985,557	2.1	—
Others	1,518,840	2.1	—
TOTAL	46,996,733	100.0	656[c]

(a)   Figures shown are nationwide percentages.

(b)   According to the ruling of the German Federal Constitutional Court, the 5 percent barrier applied in each of the two electoral districts, west and east. In east Germany, the PDS and Alliance '90 received 9.9 and 5.9 percent of votes, respectively. The western Green Party received 4.7 percent of western votes.

(c)   Because of the two-ballot nature of German elections, the actual number of Bundestag representatives will be 662. The extra members will be CDU, because that party won more direct election contests in the east than its percentage would normally have allotted it seats through the proportional representation formula.

Sources: Derived from *Deutschland Nachrichten* and *The Week in Germany*.

The 1:1 compromise leading to the exchange of east German marks for west German marks presented by Chancellor Kohl's government on April 23, 1990, endorsed by east German officials on May 2, and implemented on July 1 was a reflection of that political necessity. The exchange rate formula is presented in Table 2.2. It was designed to stem the tremendous westward stream of east Germans that caused industrial difficulties in the east and economic and political difficulties for west German governments at the national, state and local levels.

TABLE 2.2
The 1:1 Solution—
Key Exchange Rates, East German Marks for
West German Marks

1:1

     Wages and salaries
     Pensions
     Rents
     Personal savings up to 4,000 marks*

2:1

     Company debts
     Personal savings above 4,000 marks deposited as of
       December 31, 1989*
     All other monetary exchange

3:1

     Personal savings deposited after December 31, 1989

*People 60 and older were permitted to exchange 6,000 marks in personal savings at the 1:1 rate; those 14 or younger, only 2,000 marks.

Sources: The May 2 compromise as reported in the May 3, 1990, *Wall Street Journal*, p. A15, and the June 15, 1990, *Sueddeutsche Zeitung*, p. 1.

Many east Germans believed that the introduction of the DM at a 1:1 exchange rate would lead quickly to a standard of living equivalent to that in the west. Their greatest fear at the time was that their wages and pensions would be converted at a lower rate, thus immediately undermining their economic security. The 1:1 plan assuaged that particular concern but had consequences that were unforeseen by many.

That the actual conversion seemed on the surface to proceed smoothly obscured anxiety among some financial experts. One cause of their misgivings was their inability to establish how much east German cash existed outside state-sanctioned programs. Outstanding unconverted east German currency is an issue in business reorganizations, title transfers and similar transactions. At the beginning of 1991, solid data on that residue of east German marks were still not available.

Despite the Organization for Economic Cooperation and Development's (OECD) projection of German inflation rates of only 2.5 percent in 1990 and 3.25 percent in 1991, concerns about inflationary pressures will make currency an important ongoing issue. Indeed, the painful absence of reliable historical data on currency complicates the problem even further.

Another, perhaps equally important, concern of many German leaders, especially those in the Free Democratic Party (FDP), is that the currency adjustment has in some respects become politically counterproductive. It has also not allayed fears among east Germans that massive unemployment is their near-term reward for unification. Worse, nostalgia for the inefficient but reassuring cradle-to-grave social support system in the erstwhile communist territory is an obstacle to change and may well become a political motivator that could alter current party preferences.

Further, many in the German opposition believe the 1:1 rate has made unsubsidized corporate investment in eastern Germany extremely unattractive. They argue that the apparent need for considerable government support of private investment in the east is a direct economic consequence of the politically motivated July 1 monetary union. Without plentiful private sector investment and substantial governmental social security support, some SPD analysts conclude, the German government may well face renewed internal migration from east to west.

> *"One of the side effects of the monetary union is—paradoxically—the stabilization of old SED ranks in east German companies, which is a major disincentive for western investors."*
>
> Leading German
> Parliamentary Aide

COSTS OF UNIFICATION

In summer 1990, the west German government established a special "German Unity Fund" to provide a temporary borrowing mechanism. It was designed to help assure that financial assistance for the GDR would be available quickly, that such assistance would be financed equitably by the federal government and the western states, and that increased borrowing to support short-term consumption in the east would not lead to permanent tax increases for those in the west. The fund was structured to compensate for initial, limited tax-raising powers in the east, to fund eastern start-up financing for pension and unemployment insurance funds, and to begin public sector structural investment there. Table 2.3 details its borrowing plans.

It is also clear that estimates of the costs of revitalizing the east are soft at best and prone to upward revision. Substantial

TABLE 2.3
The German Unity Fund
(DM Billion)

Item	1990	1991	1992	1993	1994	Total 1990– 94
Expenditure on assistance to the GDR	22	35	28	20	10	115
Financed by:						
Borrowing by the Fund	20	31	24	15	5	95
Allocations by the federal government	2	4	4	5	5	20
Payments to meet debt service requirements	—	2.0	5.1	7.5	9.0	23.6[*]

* Debt service payments are estimated to last for another 15 to 25 years, depending on interest rate movements. They will, of course, reflect any changes in the projected expenditures reported here.

Source: *The Monthly Report of the Deutsche Bundesbank*, July 1990.

subsidies for private investment, for stabilization of wage and pension levels, for infrastructure modernization, and for environmental cleanup all combine to present a minimum public and private investment requirement that informed Germans often estimate at DM 400-750 billion over the next five years. With respect to pension levels, for example, policymakers in the GDR realized in August 1990 that pension payments for September would require some DM 3 billion in funds the FRG had granted them to cover the rest of 1990.

Additional specific estimates will continue to appear. The trend is for them to grow, partly because, for political reasons,

TABLE 2.4
Infrastructure Modernization
Estimates

	(DM Billion)
Housing	230
Roads, bridges, canals, and railroads	290
Energy and water supply	120
Environmental cleanup and monitoring	90
Telecommunications modernization	50*

* This figure, especially, varies greatly depending on the extent and sophistication of the modernizations being considered.

Sources: Institut der Deutschen Wirtschaft (Cologne), German government sources and private industry estimates.

early estimates tended to be low. The upward trend in cost estimates is already a political issue, with the SPD suggesting that early accounting by the ruling coalition was purposely unrealistic. Table 2.4 presents typical cost estimates of infrastructure modernization and identifies areas where investment is needed.

Still, public and private sector investment decisions in Germany and abroad must continually be made in spite of suspect data. Considering the comparative costs of decisions continues to be both difficult and important.

Some methods of financing unification, such as increased taxes, could slow economic growth in Germany and could conceivably have negative repercussions in the European Community. Others, such as substantial recourse to international capital markets, could raise inflation rates or international interest rates.

A sound estimate of the costs of unification would be invaluable to public and private decisionmakers. Such an estimate, however, involves a number of intangibles. The real costs of unification are those that bring the standard of living and production in the former GDR up to the levels of western Germany. But western Germany is not static. Definitions of cost therefore reflect the hopes of policymakers as well as the concrete measures that need to be taken to fix conditions in the east that all Germans agree are unsatisfactory. New information that can change such estimates becomes available daily. Even more problematic is the tendency for political priorities to change at similar rates.

Differences between east and west with respect to welfare programs, relationships between wages and benefits, guarantees associated with ownership, protection against catastrophe, and life insurance, to name a few areas, are acute. East Germans are anxious about the loss of benefits, and west Germans worry about the cost of lateral entry by east Germans into west German social welfare programs. These concerns will make personal finances a major political issue throughout the unification process.

Certainly, the strong showing of the Free Democratic Party in the December 1990 all-German election affects the direction of Kohl's plans for financing unification. At the end of 1990, the FDP strongly supported the creation of a low-tax zone in the eastern states to encourage investment. In addition, it opposed raising taxes to underwrite public spending on projects related to unification.

The balance between increased taxes, growth-inspired revenue increases and public and private investment and borrowing is not yet struck. Determining the likely division of the financial costs of unification among the German government, private industry and capital markets is a policy problem that must be attacked at the same time that a search for "accurate" estimates of such costs is under way.

In short, many economic policy decisions connected to the unification process must arise from educated guesses based on imperfect data. That type of situation does little to ease anxiety about the consequences of unification.

LAW

While east Germany was under communist control, the number of lawyers licensed to practice there was approximately 600. These lawyers were not trained to practice under the Basic Law of the Federal Republic. Further, both because their training is based on Marxism-Leninism and because their numbers are small, east German attorneys will not be able to address even a fraction of the questions that will be raised during the unification process. Among critical legal issues are civil rights, property rights (especially real estate ownership), trademarks, copyrights, and two most politically sensitive topics, taxes and abortion.

The absence of a viable legal profession in the eastern states is compounded by highly corrupted records of property ownership, unresolved claims dating back to the 1930s, and a series of quasi-legal maneuvers undertaken by the communists that have already produced a stream of protests and pleadings by victims of property seizure during the tenure of that regime. The government of the Federal Republic began before formal unification to try to devise statutes of limitation and other devices that could minimize injustice as well as confusion with regard to property ownership in the east. Tests of these devices, however, are likely to take decades. That situation alone is a major disincentive to investors who would like to establish capital plant in the east, take advantage of low labor costs

> *"Maybe the Honecker regime wasn't all bad. When Honecker departed, there were only 600 lawyers for a population of 16 million in east Germany."*
>
> A German banker

there and simultaneously ease unemployment. Investors who are discouraged will be sorely missed because they are frequently interested in providing training in modern technological methods, a service badly needed in the wake of communist economic stagnation.

BANKING

A fundamental and immediate consequence of currency adjustment was a major move by west German banks into the east. Deutsche Bank, Dresdner Bank and others led the charge. Senior officials of west German banks have been dismayed that even imaginative stopgap measures like the use of mobile telephones and fax machines fail to accommodate demand for their services in the east.

The lack of adequate communications facilities, however, proved to be only one of the problems bankers faced. Their attempts to stimulate the entrepreneurial instincts of young staff members by offering them positions in the east generally failed. Educated western Germans, in spite of differential salary increases and other incentives, proved reluctant to enter the polluted and deprived region beyond the Elbe. Eastern Germans trained in communist accounting practices proved to be of little help.

German banks as well as foreign financial services institutions from the United States and elsewhere continue to expand their services haltingly. They, like many key actors of a market economy, await decisions by the German government about whether telecommunications in the east will leapfrog existing western technologies, or whether the east will become a depository for obsolete western systems.

TELECOMMUNICATIONS

Perhaps the most graphic way to portray the present state of telecommunications in east Germany is to contrast the number of telephones in east and west Germany. In eastern Germany, only 7 percent of households have telephones; in western Germany, almost every house has one.

The switching equipment in the east is, in many cases, 50 years old. Wireline data transmission resembles that portrayed in movies about World War I. Non-wireline transmission and reception have largely been limited to the intelligence services, the military and the police. This situation is, of course, mirrored in most of the former Warsaw Pact countries.

A variety of major electronics firms, including Siemens, Ericsson, AT&T, and GE, have recognized the potential for business in the east. They have also made it clear that they are willing to invest there. The absence of decisions on development in government circles, however, slows initiatives by those firms and others interested in backing their efforts. Estimates vary, but DM 55 billion is a figure that occurs regularly in discussions about communications modernization.

One incentive for placing high priority on policy decisions with regard to telecommunications is the success of moves toward fiber-optic systems in surprising places like Warsaw and Prague. These experiments, which have involved some input from German firms as well as investment from outside the European Community, are being watched with care but have not yet precipitated licensing decisions regarding eastern Germany. The existing postal bureaucracies in Germany are the principal culprits in preventing similar moves there. Until last year, the Bundespost in west Germany and the Deutsche Post in east Germany had monopolies on telephone systems, telegraph facilities and certain data transmission networks. The merger of the two organizations is a painful bureaucratic process. Concerns over turf during the merger have done little to convince civil servants of the desirability of expanding the privatization that has already begun in western Germany.

The connections among fundamental telecommunications capability, modern banking, business practices, media, and the daily quality of human life are evident. Policy decisions, however, are extraordinarily difficult when west Germans believe that their own facilities and practices are behind the times. Legislation that would favor the economically retarded east German states in connection with telecommunications modernization will thus be difficult to draft and even more difficult to pass.

ACCOUNTANCY

Even if modern telecommunications existed, accurate data on the state of the east German economy do not. The complete distortion and accompanying inadequacy of the accounting profession in command economies is well recognized. That profession must thrive if emerging market mechanisms are to function. The ability to establish inventories, to operate reliable supply networks, to measure consumption of raw materials, and to account for labor, salaries and benefits does not exist in the east.

The absence of reliable historical accounts of east German economic performance on both the macro and the micro levels is also a severe problem. Equally important, its accounting profession currently is not equipped to monitor, measure or evaluate the effects of capital investment in the east.

A leap into very modern accounting technology and practices is possible and, many believe, desirable. It will require a training cadre from the west and an intense effort by east Germans unfamiliar with western accounting norms. A management decision to move in that direction depends in substantial measure on the emergence of a telecommunications infrastructure to support computers and on Germans' willingness to bear the cost of human investment.

MANAGEMENT

More generally, management practices of the kind we know in the west are largely absent in east Germany. Decentralized conception of objectives, competitive mobilization of resources, accurate measures of progress, and investing for the future are understood only in their most perverted forms. Key management precepts like stressing quality, customer satisfaction, new product development, and loss limitation have been stifled, if they existed at all.

Under the communist regime, accountability of managers could not be maintained. The tendency among managers was to obscure measures of performance. Managers set low goals in the first place in the hope that exceeding them would produce kudos from the party hierarchy. They adjusted goals downward seriatim when they did not meet quotas. Managerial survival was primarily a function of party connections and doctrinal orthodoxy.

The old ways will not disappear overnight. Many party functionaries remain in the residue of the communist industrial structure, insulated by their former fellow conspirators and by the very gradual practical realization among their former subordinates that a new regime may arrive.

What is known in the west as middle management—people who have acquired skills and an incentive to rise in large organizations—has not existed except within the narrow confines of party apparatus. This situation will also be difficult to disturb. Middle-aged east Germans with a decade or more of experience in a workplace where incentives did not exist are finding it difficult to adapt to notions of quality control and customer satisfaction. Many view a workplace in which performance is more important than position in a sacrosanct hierarchical structure as, at best, disturbing and, at worst, threatening.

Put succinctly, dynamic organizational cultures, encouragement of initiative, planning for creative change, and similar linchpins of western industry need to be introduced to new managers at a time when social confusion and the angst of transition as well as high unemployment make worker malleability minimal. Difficulties with law, banking and accounting further complicate managerial progress. The efforts of those attempting to establish managerial ethics and effective managerial practices, especially in large enterprises in the east, are highly constrained.

LABOR

Labor unions in western Germany participate in what often seems to some American employers an extremely foreign and unusual method of labor-management relations. This system, known as "codetermination," has as its foundation German societal consensus that industrial objectives must take into account public welfare.

Further, German workers are assured by statute that they will be granted a participatory role in decisions that affect their social welfare. Approximately 42 percent of west German workers were union members in 1988. Even nonunionized firms, however, have a works council, a board of employee representatives that must be consulted and often must approve management decisions, especially those concerning personnel and social welfare matters. In many industries, labor representatives sit on the governing boards of corporations but, in

"While you in America refer to 'labor-management relations,' we in Germany call such relations 'labor-capital relations.' This is far from an abstract difference. You imply management has an implicit right to manage workers and enterprises. We see managers as equal partners with workers."

West German labor leader

general, the exact mix of employee rights and responsibilities varies according to the size of the industry. For example, there is no requirement for codetermination in firms with fewer than five employees.

Collective bargaining in Germany is conducted outside state auspices. The state sets general minimum standards, and industry and labor reach agreements on specific matters such as workweek length and salary levels. In general, such negotiations are held between one union and one employer or employers' association, a process many Germans claim facilitates negotiation.

This differs markedly from some other western countries. Although in Germany there is often one union that negotiates for all employees in a particular industry regardless of workers' individual specialties, in other western nations several unions typically have members in a single factory. For example, a printing plant might have members from a typesetters' union, a shipping union and a white-collar union.

East German workers hope to use collective bargaining to raise wage levels to west German standards. They most likely will opt for inclusion in industrywide bargaining systems like those in the west. Many west Germans favor raising wages and working conditions to western standards because this will reduce incentives for industries to move east in search of comparative advantages.

An example is the metalwork industry. I.G. Metall, the metalworkers' union, is a leader in west German labor policy formation. A major strike by metalworkers and the printing and paper unions in 1984 led to the adoption of a standard 38.5-hour workweek in Germany. Since that time, I.G. Metall has achieved agreement on a standard 35-hour workweek, and other west German unions are following its lead. That standard is likely to prevail in the east.

I.G. Metall and other unions established dialogue with east German workers long before formal unification occurred. That dialogue was not welcomed by Communist Party leaders in the east, but it survived their discouragements. Dialogue continues but has not yet produced rapid movement in the east German workforce toward membership in existing west German unions. However, concerns among east Germans about their disadvantaged economic position may well stimulate their enthusiasm for union representation.

Nonetheless, there are obstacles. Chief among these is that east German unions and their representatives were important agents of the communist state. Many east German workers and west German union officials share an understandable mistrust of former party functionaries that has carried over in the east as suspicion of western union leaders.

It is likely that the west's codetermination system will spread eastward and that "labor-capital relations" will strongly resemble western German patterns. Of course, not all who wish to invest in eastern Germany will be enthusiastic supporters of unionization. In addition, it will take time for workers in the east to build a cadre of well-trained representatives who can work effectively within the codetermination system.

Significantly, west German labor law is being extended to the east. West German labor practices are likely to follow, although perhaps slowly, given east German workers' patterns of experience in the workplace.

WORK ETHIC

Although the German Democratic Republic has been frequently depicted as the most efficient command economy, early indications are that its workers have much to learn before they will fit into an economy organized on a market system. Many simply do not understand the requirements of such a system and the potential benefits and penalties connected with it.

Stories abound about the sometimes comical difficulties east Germans have had when trying to enter the west German workforce. Two illustrate the range of problems.

The first involves a contractor in Munich who hired east German masons from a refugee pool prior to the fall of the Berlin Wall. On their first day of employment, two masons were assigned to unload stone. They arrived on time on a Monday morning, unloaded a truckload of stone and disappeared. They were amazed when they arrived on time the next morning to find their new employer furious. In response to his wrath, they exclaimed, "How were we to know that there were seven trucks of stone coming? Where we come from, we never had more than one truck a day."

The second story involves another truant who, after an unexplained day's absence, responded to his new employer's inquiry that he did not appear the previous day because bananas were on special sale in his neighborhood and he wanted to take advantage of what for him was a rare treat. He, too, failed to understand his west German boss's choler.

These problems involving individuals suddenly immersed in a market economy suggest the huge difficulty that workers in the east will have in shifting from familiar patterns of work behavior developed over more than four decades to new patterns dimly perceived from east of the Elbe. Prolonged existence within a system in which incentives were largely absent, except for party members, will not rapidly lose its impact. Difficulties in adjustment will be most pronounced among the generations that grew into adulthood under the communist regime and labored stoically within its strictures.

Communist managers who intentionally subverted goal-setting procedures and performance measurement led by example. For more than two generations, workers in the east were conditioned to circumstances in which superior performance was regarded in most cases as subversive. Lackadaisical performance was the norm, enforced aggressively by peer pressure. Absenteeism, short workdays and other maladies common in command economies afflicted east German enterprises.

These work practices must be taken into account during the transition to a market system. However, productivity, quality, competitiveness, incentives based on differential wages, and personal responsibility are concepts not grasped quickly. Training, education and sustained experience are necessary if economic transformation is to succeed.

CULTURAL INTEGRATION

Although generations may pass before east and west Germans agree on historical facts and interpretations, the process of unification is aided by a common language and basic culture. The older generation remembers basic German values like industry, ingenuity and conscientiousness. Younger generations in the east will no longer be force-fed Marxist-Leninist distortions of those values. An educational system built on the tenets of the Basic Law will reinforce the notion of responsible citizenship and help in the transition toward work practices consistent with market economics.

Energetic attempts by the communist regime to fracture the nuclear family were only partially successful. Still, differences between family, lifestyle and organization in east and west are significant. For example, under the communist system, almost all east German women of working age were employed. They required, and were granted, access to free or inexpensive child care. The need to search and perhaps pay for child care will be keenly felt by women whose incomes may now be essential to the financial stability of their families.

Abortion rights, women's rights, divorce, and the economic necessity of maintaining two-income households are relatively dormant political issues at present. They were discussed to some degree during the months preceding unification, but the more immediate issues of employment opportunities, job security, unemployment insurance, taxes, and pension benefits outweighed them in the public consciousness. Still, many basic societal differences on less critical issues were papered over in the unification treaty. They may emerge again with some force as the difficulties of social convergence become increasingly visible.

Also, in spite of the best efforts of the communists, religion never died in the east. Religious leaders were prominent in the moves toward liberation and formal unification. Dialogue among coreligionists in east and west can help erode the distance that evolved between the two Germanies.

The electronics media were another significant factor in political developments leading toward unification. Access to west German television and to other western sources of information allowed east Germans to develop an awareness and, later, an urgency about their deprived lifestyle.

Media in communist regimes have traditionally been used to reinforce orthodoxy. Advertising, entertainment and independent news reporting now readily available to east Germans may help them better understand notions of competitiveness and, more generally, the day-to-day lifestyle of their western counterparts.

The liberating and motivating impact of information should not be underestimated. Telephones, radio and television, copying machines, facsimile machines, and personal computers are but a few technologies that could aid east Germans in adjusting politically and economically to western standards of individual freedom and incentive-based economic activity.

ENERGY

The principal source of energy for east German industry has been soft coal. (Charts 2.2 and 2.3 portray the primary sources of energy consumption in east and west Germany, respectively.) Auxiliary sources for east Germany have been Soviet oil and Soviet natural gas. In 1988, the USSR supplied 87 percent of the GDR's imported oil. Soviet gas became available through a highly controversial pipeline deal in the mid-1980s that extended Soviet distribution systems across east Germany into western Europe.

The dependency question then raised in NATO and EC circles and especially in Washington has not been resolved. Any economy that counts on Soviet supply risks proportional political pressure on its leaders when they disagree with Soviet authorities. The tenuous future of those authorities and of the Soviet Union itself must also remain a matter of concern.

So far, the Soviets have several reasons for wanting to continue as an energy supplier to the east German economy. One is access to hard currency. Another is that the expensive natural gas infrastructure that services both east Germans and customers farther west is operating at only 40 percent of capacity.

CHART 2.2
East German Primary Energy Consumption, 1988

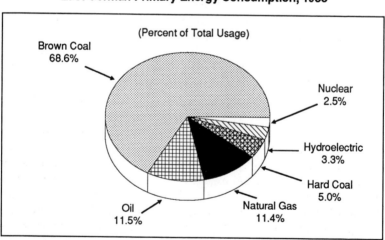

Note: Figures do not equal 100 percent due to the lack in precision of East German statistics.

Source: Institut der Deutschen Wirtschaft (Cologne).

CHART 2.3
West German Primary Energy Consumption, 1989

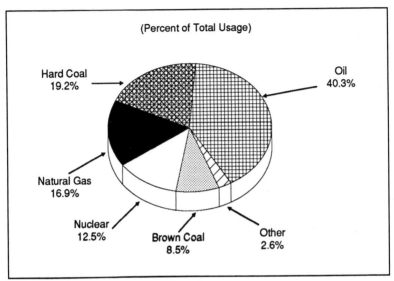

(Percent of Total Usage)

Hard Coal
19.2%

Oil
40.3%

Natural Gas
16.9%

Nuclear
12.5%

Brown Coal
8.5%

Other
2.6%

Source: Institut der Deutschen Wirtschaft (Cologne).

This low figure is partly the result of the west's reluctance to provide modern pumps and compressors to the Soviet Union, stemming from a lack of enthusiasm for ruble transactions as well as from concerns about technology transfer.

Existing coal-consuming energy production facilities in east Germany would appear on the surface to be capable of fairly rapid modification that would improve plant efficiency and reduce energy production costs. Unfortunately, most experts agree that the age and disrepair of east German plant makes conversion impractical financially and undesirable environmentally.

A theoretical alternative to Soviet natural gas and to brown coal could be nuclear power. However, western experts fully familiar with Chernobyl are amazed that an accident occurred in the Soviet Union before an even larger-scale disaster happened in east Germany. One of the early policy decisions in the wake of unification was to close most east German nuclear plants. Again, most energy specialists familiar with existing east German nuclear facilities deem retrofitting extremely unwise.

Excess energy from other European sources, including the French electrical system and relatively low cost oil and natural gas supplies from the North Sea, may be important in the period of transition from existing to modern systems in eastern Germany. Similarly, the Soviet hunger for deutsche marks may produce a buyers' market for a combined Germany in the short term for both petroleum and natural gas.

Modernization of energy production is an extraordinarily capital-intensive undertaking. But problems do not end there. Energy transmission systems in the east are obsolete and economically unsound targets for rehabilitation. Further, both production and transmission facilities must be developed in a way that takes into account ecological sensitivity.

Basically, then, the energy infrastructure in east Germany is a prime target for massive infusion of western capital and technology. The necessity to inject consumer service orientation at the same time that policymakers deal with cost, hardware and ecological considerations makes managing the energy sector a problem of the first order.

ECOLOGICAL FACTORS

It is striking that Germany, a nation noted for its sensitivity to nature and its concern for environmental quality, should find itself faced with a grotesque example of ecological criminality. The communist government of the GDR ravaged the country's air, soil and water.

In some eastern industrial areas, life expectancy is five years lower than the average in the region at large. Some of those areas almost never see the sun. Air and water pollution endanger life. Some of the reasons for this destruction include: flawed energy production systems skewed toward supplying industries at almost any environmental cost; socialist industrial systems that encouraged the maintenance of obsolete technologies and plant; inadequate enforcement of those environmental protection regulations that did exist; and official secrecy about environmental damage.

Despite the emergence of very strong "green" sentiments in both Germanies (most advocates of the green position argue that it originated in east Germany), the east German communist regime took essentially no account of environmental devastation created by obsolete industrial practices. The consequences of long-term environmental neglect make attempts to remedy the existing deleterious conditions throughout east Germany extremely challenging and extraordinarily expensive. Paradoxically, the severity of the environmental damage now being widely recognized in east Germany may provide an argument for leaping technological generations in terms of production and for investing profits from more efficient production in a cleanup effort that could employ spinoffs of the same high technology.

> *"Forty years of central economic planning wrought massive environmental destruction in the former GDR. Nature was plundered and concerns for human health were wantonly neglected. . . . Flowing rivers have turned into bodies of stagnant water, clean air has turned into filthy, noxious smog, and soil has been poisoned. We in the west must strain to imagine the enormity of the pollution."*
>
> Professor Klaus Toepfer,
> Federal Minister for the Environment

The Luddite tendencies of the Green movement are no minor disincentive to foreign investment in the depressed east. Every new investment in industry there will be scrutinized locally from an environmental standpoint in a way that might well slow economic development. In addition, the day-to-day trauma of east German citizens in terms of breathable air, potable water and hopes for an attractive landscape in which to raise their children are political factors that are not negligible and that may have more impact in the east than they currently have in the west.

AGRICULTURE

Roughly 11 percent of the east German population is involved in agriculture. Much of the agricultural activity is collective in nature, reflecting not only Leninist economic precepts, but also the peasant-landowner relationship that preceded the arrival of the communist regime.

Farms in eastern Germany are very large and yet less productive than are those in western Germany. Estimates vary, but most western experts agree that west German farmers are currently about twice as productive as their eastern counterparts.

EC agricultural policies are of great importance to Germany because of the Federal Republic's stake in maintaining current supports for farmers. Adding the productive capability of east Germany to Federal Republic production levels has made Germany an even more formidable force in internal EC agricultural negotiations.

The conditions negotiated for east German accession into the European Community and the Common Agricultural Policy (CAP) may be a sticking point in the consolidation of the east and west German economies. Further, disputes over the level and distribution of agricultural support within the EC could lead to disputes between Germany and other EC members and between the EC and other world agricultural exporters.

Some observers fear that Germany might become a stronger advocate of the EC's Common Agricultural Policy than it would have been absent unification. After all, agricultural interest groups in Germany possessed considerable domestic political influence even before unification. Eastern Germany has a sizable agricultural sector that could add its influence to the weight of western farmers in domestic and EC discussions of farm reform. One example that could be cited of such potential for international complications is the General Agreement on Tariffs and Trade (GATT) negotiations on agriculture. Unification and the tensions that accompanied it, especially as east German farmers found few markets for their goods, left German leaders little room to maneuver among domestic, EC and international goals for reforming trade in farm products.

Other observers argue that increased inner-EC friction over the cost of the CAP may result if east German farm production lives up to its potential. They conclude that such friction may actually be in the U.S. interest if it leads to a reform of the CAP. Such hypothetical benefits, however, seemed dim at the end of 1990 as tensions over EC domestic agricultural supports and export subsidies played an important role in the suspension of the GATT round of negotiations.

It will make considerable difference to German farmers whether their eventual share of total EC agricultural production is set at current levels of west German production, at current levels of east and west German production, at production levels that east Germany could achieve with modern farming methods, or at levels linked to east German consumption of agricultural goods. If the accession of east Germany to the EC leads to a net increase in agricultural goods produced, the export of those goods at subsidized prices will only accentuate the tension between the United States and the European Community.

TRANSPORTATION

Since World War II, major air, rail, land, and water routes have developed within the two blocs, not between them. The prospect of connecting existing capabilities and regularizing operating procedures is daunting at best.

Eastern German commercial air capabilities are obsolete, and air traffic control problems make commercial expansion marginally safe. Roads, railways and canals exist generally in the conditions that prevailed in west Germany in the 1950s. East German ports along the Baltic are similarly anachronistic.

Cost estimates for improving east German transportation infrastructure vary greatly. Optimists believe that at least DM 200 billion will be required to bring east German facilities up to the standards presently existing in the west.

Modern design and construction techniques applied to transportation problems could result in both economies of scale and rapid improvements in the east. Capital infusion is the key ingredient. Successful application of capital, however, will depend once again on managerial capacity and workforce reformation.

In addition, the quality of east German transportation networks is generally acknowledged to be abysmal. It will be necessary to spend significantly to build rail and road networks that facilitate integration as well as commerce. The relation between public and private sector activities in these pursuits raises political questions that have already proved thorny in the west.

TAXATION

Extension of existing tax structures from west to east is complicated by a variety of factors, including the necessity to establish accounting, reporting and collection capabilities there. Connecting those capabilities to computerized western data banks is also no mean task.

In spite of wage differentials, stubborn problems associated with corporate structures, and the embryonic development of banking in the east, public acceptance of west German tax practices in the east seems certain. Implementation of compliance mechanisms will be slow, but negative political fallout in that connection does not seem to be a prospect.

The principal political difficulties of taxation are likely to emerge when it becomes more evident that the population of the west is providing a disproportionate share of the funding for eastern modernization. The private sector/public sector balance in terms of modernization costs is still evolving, but there is no question that the public sector must take the lead. Creation and implementation of development policy with regard to the east is probably the most fractious issue facing the unified German government in the near term.

The parameters of the debate remain to be defined. However, it is clear from opposition statements that the SPD challenge to the existing coalition will have at its center painful questions about the distribution of financial burdens across the German population. Related questions about distribution of financial resources have already proved politically volatile.

EMPLOYMENT

The transformation of the east German economy involves massive dislocations in the workforce. At the end of September 1990, nearly a quarter of the approximately 9 million east German workers were unemployed or on short-time work. The numbers of unemployed continued to escalate as 1990 ended. In December, there were 600,000 unemployed in eastern Germany and more than 1.8 million workers on short-time work. (See Table 2.5.)

The reason for this unemployment, simply put, is that the number of jobs lost because of collapse of east German firms is not being matched by creation of new employment opportunities there. To make matters worse, the prosperous west is running at nearly full industrial capacity, removing an additional possibility for unemployed eastern workers to find positions there.

Creation of modern plant, expansion of service industries and other moves likely to alleviate east German unemployment in the medium term await adjustments in infrastructure previously outlined. In the interim, the potential for poverty, despair and even desperation in the east German workforce is a politically explosive factor.

TABLE 2.5
East German Labor Market Data, 1990
(Thousands)

Month	Vacancies	Short-Time Workers	Unemployed	UE Rate (%)
JAN	158.6	—	7.4	0.1
FEB	141.4	—	11.0	0.1
MAR	105.9	—	38.3	0.4
APR	73.6	—	64.9	0.7
MAY	54.3	—	94.8	1.1
JUN	41.4	—	142.1	1.6
JUL	27.7	656.3	272.0	3.1
AUG	20.4	1,499.6	361.3	4.1
SEP	24.4	1,771.6	444.8	5.0

Source: *Monthly Report of the Deutsche Bundesbank*, October 1990.

The continued presence of so-called guest workers is an additional complication. These workers, generally Turks in the west and Vietnamese in the east, are employed in relatively unskilled jobs that could provide subsistence for east Germans during the period of economic transition accompanying unification. Clear policy decisions on these workers are connected inexorably to the overall question of the permeability of borders. Refugees from east European countries can be counted on to look toward the European Community in general and Germany in particular as potential safe havens from economic despair.

Some of these refugees are, or at least were, culturally German. Their exodus from Poland, Hungary, Czechoslovakia, and elsewhere may well receive added impetus if emigration from the Soviet Union westward continues to increase.

The human dimension of economic transformation forces attention to stark political realities. The pace of economic change in Germany is unlikely to meet the expectations of its less privileged citizens. The capacity of the German economy to absorb immigrants will be extremely limited for a substantial period.

Further, the difficulties that unification is creating for east German professionals are numerous. For example, medical personnel in the east, conscientious and skilled though they may be, are decades behind those in the west in terms of their knowledge of diagnostic technologies, modern equipment, sanitation, and similar improvements in medical practice enjoyed in the west. They face the prospect of expensive and time-consuming retraining if they are to update facilities and practices in the east.

Their difficulties illustrate the overall restriction on mobility of professionals in a variety of occupations. Steep learning curves retard their capacity to move westward. Limited resources and a limited knowledge base are slowing their ability to modernize. Morale problems, especially among middle-aged professionals trying to face these difficulties, are inevitable.

How German leaders choose to deal with these troublesome realities will be an important element in the reputation they acquire as sensitive and generous leaders in the democratic west. Equally important, there is no question that Germany will be the principal player in whatever evolution occurs on its eastern borders. Its central position in Europe makes Germany a principal focus of concern for all its neighbors.

OUTLOOK

The collapse of the east German system and the difficulty of identifying aspects of it that are worthy of being adopted by a united Germany will probably lead many east Germans to feel inferior, at least in the near term. East Germans insist they should enjoy the same social welfare benefits as do west Germans. This strong desire is in part a manifestation of their determination to move through the unification process as a partner, albeit junior, rather than as a supplicant.

Resentment against east German immigrants is growing in the west. Lateral entry of east Germans into existing west German social welfare programs is often perceived in the west to be unfair. The influx of immigrants from east Germany has tightened housing markets, creating difficulties for west Germans. The aftereffects of the currency exchange are yet to be measured. Indeed, the overall cost of unification will continue to be a stringent political issue.

Germans on both sides fear that they will have to bear a disproportionate share of the costs of unification. Thus, the potential for intense political friction and even for significant social unrest is present as unification proceeds.

It would be a mistake, however, to draw a conclusion based entirely on difficulties in the unification process. Germany possesses immense resources—human, fiscal and material—that it can use in solving the kinds of problems previously outlined. Equally important, Germany does not stand alone. Its commitment to the European Community not only reassures its neighbors, but also opens the door for the cooperation, consideration and general goodwill necessary to allow the various adjustments Germans are likely to have to make.

The European Community is an environment that will foster German economic development. The changing security structures in Europe are likely to continue to provide Germans with assurance of physical safety and reinforce the tendency of that country to view itself as an integral element in the west.

Change within Germany is dramatic. But undue concentration by Americans on the domestic difficulties inherent in the unification process is ill-advised. Germany's future and the future of U.S.-German relations are conditioned in substantial measure by the position that Germany will have in the economic and security structures of the west. These external considerations are the focus of the next chapters.

CHAPTER THREE

Germany's International Economic Environment

The role that Germany develops for itself within Europe and in the wider world economy should be of great concern to the United States. Germany's political decisions will in the future influence U.S. foreign and domestic stability and security to a far greater degree than they have since the end of World War II. Germany is an established economic superpower and is gaining influence rapidly in political and security fora. Germany is the economic leader of the European Community, a body currently developing greater cohesion in foreign, trade, monetary, and security policies and capable of influencing world events in a manner that, until recently, only the United States could effect.

According to the European Commission, EC states received 53 percent of U.S. manufacturers' overseas investment in 1989. American firms also spent more on mergers and acquisitions in Europe in 1989 than did firms of any EC state. American corporations have invested over $130 billion in EC firms and employ more than 2 million people in Europe. The ties between the United States and Europe are significant and long-term. The fact that Germany's role in the EC is becoming more pivotal has important ramifications for individuals and companies that have investments or operations in the EC.

That Germany is now unified significantly changes its relative strength. Germany's postwar development as an economic and political leader had been gradual and continuous, but has now taken a great leap in strength and pace. Most of the Federal Republic's partners have become accustomed to strong but tactful German international economic influence. Few were prepared for the surge in German political power caused by the events of 1989 and 1990.

Unification has accelerated Germany's influence both because the country has become larger and more powerful and because many of Germany's allies are anxious to guarantee that their concerns and interests will continue to be considered by German policymakers. Germany's partners in the international economic system have a number of concrete worries about unification processes and about the effects that changing German policies will have on the European Community, international capital markets, exchange rates, foreign investment, trade flows, and the GATT.

The dissolution of the Soviet empire in central Europe may slightly modulate the values and principles that guided German policies in the postwar era. However, the massive political changes of 1989-90 have definitely altered the index of issues Federal Republic policymakers traditionally tended to consult as well as how national priorities are likely to be ranked in the future.

Unification and the conditions that brought it about also have altered the evolution of the European Community. Progress toward the Community's single market prior to unification, especially since 1986, has been astonishing compared with the "Eurosclerosis" of the 1970s and early 1980s. But the number and scope of internal issues EC members are facing have increased dramatically in 1989 and 1990. Further, the problems that countries in emancipated eastern Europe have raised for Community members, especially Germany, are already numerous and will increase.

German preoccupation with issues arising from unification is undeniable, but could well last only a few years. Some sort of eastern German "economic miracle" cannot be ruled out. The consequences of relatively short-term introspection, however, may have much longer-term repercussions on the deepening and widening of the European Community as well as on the shaping of the post-Cold War international economy. Germany will be making many important, perhaps irreversible, political and economic decisions in the next few years.

GERMAN POWER AND EUROPEAN QUESTIONS

Since World War II, Germany has developed into a trading state that benefits substantially from its close economic and political ties within the west. The Marshall Plan provided the seed money for postwar reconstruction in Europe. The development of such institutions as the European Coal and Steel Community (ECSC) and the European Economic Community helped Germany's economy first to rebuild and later to prosper. Table 3.1 illustrates that the majority of German trade is now with other EC member states, of which Germany has merchandise trade surpluses with all but Ireland. As German exports slow and imports rise because of increased demand in Germany, the other EC nations are likely to profit from any reversal in their balance of trade with Germany.

Germany's health as a trading state is dependent on the health of its EC partners' economies. Approximately 55 percent of Germany's exports and 51 percent of its imports were traded with EC members in 1989. Germany is highly suited to compete in European and world markets and has every reason to pursue policies that will further the comparative economic strength of the Community.

Many Germans seem convinced that the EC's progress toward eventual political and economic union is a necessary condition for the prosperity of the European Community. Progress toward "EC 1992" and the general economic prosperity of the middle and late 1980s have encouraged such optimism. In any event, the unification of Germany has intensified the political rhetoric leading to closer European union.

In late 1989, few in Europe, and even fewer outsiders, would have credited the concept of an Inter-governmental Conference (IGC) charged with rewriting the 1957 Treaty of Rome's provisions for political union. Economic prosperity and German unification became driving forces behind the popularity of a more unified European Community. German leaders have stated their determination to anchor their nation's unification in a larger European context. That position enjoys broad support among the German population. Germany's neighbors are clearly not displeased with the sentiment, but the likely relative

TABLE 3.1
German Trade with EC Members
(U.S.$ Million)

		1987	1988	1989
Belgium/	exports	21,686	24,008	24,463
Luxembourg	imports	16,244	17,777	18,604
	balance	5,442	6,231	5,859
Denmark	exports	6,228	6,431	6,544
	imports	4,283	4,723	4,924
	balance	1,945	1,708	1,620
France	exports	35,479	40,647	44,910
	imports	26,495	30,271	32,208
	balance	8,984	10,376	12,702
Greece	exports	2,759	3,150	3,427
	imports	1,878	1,822	1,817
	balance	881	1,328	1,610
Ireland	exports	1,286	1,391	1,584
	imports	1,966	2,086	2,328
	balance	−680	−695	−744
Italy	exports	25,705	29,461	31,853
	imports	21,859	22,934	24,072
	balance	3,846	6,527	7,781
Nether-	exports	25,705	28,035	28,968
lands	imports	25,060	25,932	27,675
	balance	645	2,103	1,293
Portugal	exports	2,069	2,605	2,954
	imports	1,587	1,756	2,127
	balance	482	849	827
Spain	exports	8,400	10,215	11,892
	imports	4,561	5,120	5,658
	balance	3,839	5,095	6,234
United Kingdom	exports	25,748	30,093	31,573
	imports	16,291	17,355	18,483
	balance	9,457	12,738	13,090

Source: Derived from *Direction of Trade Statistics Yearbook 1990* (International Monetary Fund), p. 134.

increase in German economic leverage within the EC does little
to comfort many, especially the French.

The political notion of "Europe" may currently be as important to Germany as its economic ties. United Germany, because
of 20th-century German actions in Europe, cannot afford to use
intensive nationalistic appeals for sacrifice on the part of east
and west Germans to make unification work. The historical parallels that might be drawn from such appeals could alienate
Germans and their neighbors who have an acute sense of history. Germans are generally confident, however, that market
forces will prevail without endangering their democratic political system.

As the European Community has developed, Germany has
worked within it to further its national and international interests. This process has long roots and has grown stronger and
more productive in recent years. By working with other
Community members, especially France, to form and enact policies, Germany has been able to appear relatively subtle and
self-effacing in international negotiations, while at the same
time achieving many of its goals. This has involved using the
special French-German relationship to reach compromises that
the two countries can later advocate together on the Community
level.

This method of operation has worked well within the western European frame. France and Germany have many goals in
common, and the Germans have tended until recently to encourage the French to take the political lead in advocating such common policies. This apparent subordination of national interests
to supranational interests has served Germany well.

In the short term—perhaps until January 1993—the current goals aimed at strengthening economic and social bonds
among EC members should work easily in tandem with German
political interests. EC goals such as moving toward monetary
union, harmonizing differing legal systems and achieving a single market are generally referred to as deepening. This term is
also sometimes used to suggest further surrender of "sovereign
prerogatives" like control over foreign or defense policies. The
term widening is usually used in contrast to deepening.
Widening the Community refers to increasing its membership.

The two terms are typically used in sentences that illustrate
the potential conflicts between admitting new members to the
EC and strengthening the supranational and institutional

bonds that hold together the present 12 members. In time, particularly after January 1, 1993, the EC will likely admit new members. Even before that time, it is likely to make considerable progress toward concluding association and cooperation agreements with other European states. Despite current angst over sovereign and fiscal consequences of monetary union and sovereign and political consequences of security and political union, deepening will likely proceed as well, although probably at a much slower pace than the events of 1990 would portend. The European reaction, or rather the differing reactions of individual EC nations, to the war in the Persian Gulf in early 1991 serves to underline that progress on economic unity will be easier for the EC than will formal security or political unity.

Deepening the Community within the limits of the 1992 program that are outlined below may even serve to justify a tax increase in Germany in the name of harmonizing EC member states' value-added-tax (VAT) rates. VAT rates in Germany are low in comparison with many other EC nations (see Table 3.2). An increase in German VAT rates could be made in the name of European unity and the single market. That such an adjustment might help to pay part of the bill for German unification makes such a move no less desirable in political circles in that country.

THE "EC 1992" PROGRAM

Germany's political and economic outlook is best understood in the context of EC development. The European Community, established in 1957 by 6 states, now has 12 members (see Table 3.3). In June 1985, the European Commission issued a white paper titled *Completing the Internal Market*. That document, signed by member states in 1986, provided the framework and a deadline of December 31, 1992, for a program of near-complete Community economic integration. Member states' public and private acceptance of the goal of Community economic integration, referred to in common parlance as "EC 1992," has led to a dynamic revitalization of European commerce and the idea of "Europe" as a workable community.

The business community's confidence in the EC 1992 program has led to a resurgence of trade and increased capital investment within the Community. According to Commission statistics, intra-Community trade, in constant decline between

TABLE 3.2
VAT Rates in EC Countries
(Percent as of July 1990)

Country	Lower Rates[*]	Standard Rates	Higher Rates
Belgium	1, 6, 17	19	25, 33
Denmark	—	22	—
France	2.1, 4.5, 5.5, 13	18.6	25
Germany	7	14	—
Greece	8	18	36
Ireland	0, 2.4, 10	23	—
Italy	2, 9	18	38
Luxembourg	3, 6	12	—
Netherlands	6	18.5	—
Portugal	0, 8	16	30
Spain	6	12	33
United Kingdom	0	15	—

[*] Excluding some minor goods with zero ratings and exemptions, which in some countries account for a substantial part of total consumption, but which would require substantial space for documentation here. Rates vary according to the type of item offered for sale.

Source: *Taxation and International Capital Flows* (Paris: OECD, June 1990), p. 161.

1973 and 1985, has risen to nearly 62 percent of member state exports, a high figure not seen since a peak in the early 1970s.

The OECD reports that average gross fixed capital formation for EC countries grew 10.4 percent in 1988 over the previous year and 9.1 percent more in 1989 than in 1988. Comparable figures for the United States are 8.4 percent in 1988 and 4.1 percent in 1989. Since 1984, EC industrial output has grown 20 percent. Community growth in investment,

TABLE 3.3
EC Membership Growth

1957	Belgium
	France
	Germany
	Italy
	Luxembourg
	Netherlands
1973	Denmark
	United Kingdom
	Ireland
1981	Greece
1986	Portugal
	Spain

employment and trade reflects not only the general economic upswing of the mid-1980s, but also larger viable markets and stiffer competition for its goods and services within the EC. In addition, its businesses' anticipation of their improving capability to compete globally has reinforced enthusiasm for the EC.

Today's state of affairs could not have emerged without the passage in 1985 of the Single European Act by the EC Council of Ministers. Until passage of that act, a unanimous vote by the Council was required to ratify decisions on proposals offered to the Council by the Community's executive bureaucracy. The Single European Act currently allows a "weighted majority" vote on many important matters to convey binding approval on policy questions.

The Single European Act supplies the necessary foundation for, but does not guarantee the achievement of:

- completion of the internal Community market by January 1, 1993;

- development of a Community social policy;

- creation of a technical and research community;

- closer harmonization of environmental policy among member states;

- enhancement of the authority of Community institutions; and

- expansion of EC cooperation in security and foreign policy-making.

The act does not, however, mandate the use of majority voting on issues of taxation and internal border checks on people, or on "measures relating to the rights and interests of employed persons."

The near-term EC goal for the single market is complete removal of remaining physical, technical and fiscal barriers to trade within the Community. These barriers to a free internal market include border controls on goods and people, controls on the movement of capital, restrictions on cross-border financial and other services, public procurement differences, differing technical standards, and nationally varying taxation and legal systems.

COMMUNITY SOCIAL POLICY

The Single European Act also provided for the development of a Community social policy. The intent was to counter claims that the 1992 program would benefit businesses at the expense of workers. Early in 1989, the Commission proposed a draft charter of basic social rights. Little progress has been made in refining charter provisions. The core of Community steps toward a social policy is the Action Program of the Social Charter. This program proposes more than 70 EC-wide laws to improve social conditions. These include rights such as improved living and working conditions, a maximum workweek for all workers regardless of occupation, free movement of labor, harmonization of the right to residence in all member states, vocational training, equality of the sexes, freedom of association, collective bargaining and trade union formation, worker participation in management decisions, health and safety protection, and a Community-wide minimum work age of 16.

The United Kingdom, in particular, has been concerned that the continental system of worker-capital relations might replace Britain's freer market system. National and international trade union organizations are working with member governments and the Commission to determine the appropriate mix of Community and national regulation of social issues.

The German Trade Union Federation favors the political and economic union of Europe but has expressed concern that progress on the EC Social Charter has taken a back seat to market deregulation measures. One of the DGB's major concerns is that not enough has been done to broaden organized labor's rights of participation in and consultation with the institutions of the Community. Although the Social Democratic group in the European Parliament has expressed similar concerns to Jacques Delors, President of the European Commission, the Federation is somewhat disappointed with the Parliament's seemingly lukewarm commitment to the Social Charter. Delors, for his part, has said that "liberalization and harmonization go hand in hand."

The DGB continues to express its belief that the Social Charter process will raise overall European labor standards without decreasing social standards in the north to the lower levels more common in southern Europe. Continued migration from eastern Europe may change the unions' outlooks if substantial numbers of workers willing to be paid lower salaries enter the German labor market.

GERMANY AND THE 1992 PROGRAM

The German government's support for progress on 1992 initiatives has been steady. Chancellor Kohl in particular has been at the forefront of recent proposals for quick action to achieve political as well as economic union. He has also stressed that popular German support for integrative programs is a manifestation of the German determination to be "European Germans." At the spring 1989 summit of the EC Council in Dublin, he stated his "urgent wish for all Europeans to believe that German unity and European integration are two sides of the same coin." Many see Kohl's support of the EC's GATT negotiating position on agricultural subsidies as a reflection of his determination to put European interests at the forefront of Germany's economic agenda.

Among the EC topics of greatest interest to Germany are the controls on government supports for industries, the Common Agricultural Policy, and hedges against a surge of protectionist sentiment within the Europe of the Twelve. Germany, the leading trading state in the Community, is understandably interested in market liberalization. However, it is reluctant unilaterally to sacrifice government supports for certain economic sectors. For example, Kohl's political coalition receives much of the farm vote in Germany. Predictably, he is concerned with influencing the CAP reform discussions that began in January 1991. Germany also has a strong interest in discouraging EC protectionism lest reciprocity damage German exports. In general, German leaders play down the fractiousness of these issues and emphasize Germany's history of sympathy toward EC initiatives.

Even prior to unification, German economic growth mandated a growing political role for Germany within the 1992 program. The program is intended to increase coordination of economic, and therefore to some extent political, decisionmaking and planning among the 12 member nations. Success to date has led many Community leaders to reach toward greater monetary, and even political, cooperation. Germany, already arbiter of currency in Europe and simultaneously gaining in comparative advantage by almost any economic measure, faces a dilemma. To use its strengths in the unification process, it must be assertive in EC deliberations. To be a "European Germany," it may have to subordinate its domestic concerns. German leaders, especially Kohl, must constantly calculate the political consequences of such solomonic choices.

THE COMMON AGRICULTURAL POLICY

Many Europeans have long supported the CAP in part because it can be seen as a symbol of European integration. Within the EC, with the possible exception of the United Kingdom, there is broad general agreement that the CAP is worth keeping in some revised form. Post-1992, however, the CAP's value as a symbol of EC integration will be much diminished. In addition, many believe the negative publicity the CAP attracted in the wake of the December 1990 disagreements in the GATT negotiations has damaged the EC's international image.

The CAP is designed to maintain internal EC prices for agricultural products at artificially high levels by imposing a flexible tariff on agricultural imports and by subsidizing exports of surplus commodities. The amount of the tariff on imports fluctuates, but it is roughly equal to the difference between the EC support price and the price of imports. Thus, imports can only fill demand that exceeds what EC farmers produce. The CAP has few production controls (major examples are dairy controls and the mechanism for stabilizing grain prices). Surplus farm goods are subsidized for export at world competitive prices or lower.

In 1989, the CAP cost EC taxpayers and consumers an estimated $93 billion. The EC's budget for supporting agriculture is approximately two-thirds of the entire EC budget. Yet agricultural goods account for less than 5 percent of Community GDP. The inclusion of east Germany in the CAP is likely to result in increased expenditures if its share of EC agricultural production is placed at levels that can be achieved with modern farming methods. Increasing budgetary pressures resulting from the accession of largely agricultural east Germany are not likely to ease political or economic tensions within the EC, especially during negotiations on reforming the CAP.

Since the 1970s, the United States and the EC have been engaged in a steadily escalating subsidies war that has dramatically affected the world market price for farm products. At first, differences between these two largest agricultural blocs were mainly over the degree of U.S. access to the EC market, but as the EC became a net exporter of agricultural products, the central dispute shifted to issues arising from U.S. and EC competition in third-country markets.

The intensity of this conflict was reflected in the complications accompanying what was supposed to be the concluding meeting of the GATT Uruguay Round in December 1990. Differences between the EC and the United States over the liberalization of trade in agricultural products were arguably the underlying reason those concluding talks collapsed. That agricultural issues could serve as a catalyst reflects their important place in the international trade negotiations themselves as well as their political and economic impacts on those countries that export or import significant quantities of agricultural products.

LEADERSHIP WITHIN THE EC

The events of 1989 and 1990 have pushed Germany into a more visible position as leader in the EC. Anxiety about German predominance within Europe helps to explain French moves in 1989 and 1990 toward the type of political coordination de Gaulle would promptly have terminated.

Within the European Community, France has traditionally been the political spokesman, while Germany has led in the economic sphere. As long as Germany was content to let France speak for it, and as long as German and French interests converged, this situation was unlikely to change. But Germany's political reticence existed in spite of its economic strength, which should have granted it greater political leverage in a largely economic association of nations.

For much of the first half of the 20th century, German actions caused all its neighbors misery. Many in Germany believe that it has had to pay penance for its actions in World War II by being as low key as possible in the international political realm. After the war, Germany developed and articulated many of its national interests within supranational bodies. NATO and the EC have been safety nets allowing Germany to work through the policies of others or through joint policies while still playing an active part in the international scene.

Containing Germany has been a major French postwar goal. German cooperation within the European Community has been a primary instrument. As long as the Federal Republic's ability to influence events in eastern Europe was constricted by Soviet influence, French and German interests tended to converge. Now, Germany and not France, for reasons of geography and economic performance if not of history or cultural sensitivity, has emerged as the model for east European states.

Simultaneously, united Germany is emerging as *primus inter pares* in the European Community—largely at the expense of France. It occupies a central geographic position in Europe. It has Europe's strongest economy. It arguably has Europe's most successful monetary policy. And, it is free of the restrictions on its sovereignty that emerged from World War II.

Germany increasingly will want to enjoy the international standing that the success of its political and economic systems merits. For a variety of reasons—fewer external constraints on sovereign actions, greater diplomatic prestige and the influence that follows, and a surfeit of "vital interests"—German rhetoric is likely to become more direct. German policy preferences are likely to be articulated more forcefully. And, German reticence in comparing Germany's economic program with those of others will disappear. These developments provide major challenges for German diplomats trying to minimize anxiety and resentment among Germany's neighbors and friends.

COMMUNITY INSTITUTIONAL DEVELOPMENT

Despite German rhetoric in support of Community integration, German domestic priorities sometimes conflict with consensus EC decisions. The EC has made a great deal of progress since 1985 in moving toward a single integrated market, but it is still a community of nation-states. Responsibilities that are "federal" in the United States (monetary, fiscal, defense, and foreign policies) are currently largely under the control of individual member states in the EC. A brief look at the structure of the EC is a helpful step toward understanding how Germany fits into that environment.

The EC Council of Ministers is presently the principal decisionmaking body in the EC. It is composed of ministers from the governments of member countries who consider proposals of the EC Commission and may pass them into law as is, amend them or reject them. During this process, the Council is charged to take into account the views of the European Parliament. (When the Council meets, the press frequently refers to the gathering as an "EC summit.")

Under the weighted majority system of voting in the Council introduced by the Single European Act, the United Kingdom, France, Italy, and Germany have the most votes. This provision of the act, covering most, although not all, decisions on single market legislation, means that one nation can no longer veto directives unilaterally. For a directive to be rejected by the Council, two large countries and one small country, one large country and three small countries, or various combinations of small countries must vote against it.

It has been rare for German Council ministers to be anything but highly cooperative in working to achieve EC objectives. That situation is unlikely to change quickly as German economic influence in Europe increases.

In a move toward rationalization, regularization and, inevitably, centralization of decisionmaking, the Single European Act has facilitated passage of EC directives by majority vote of the Council. The December 1990 Council summit in Rome moved to eliminate additional barriers against common EC monetary and foreign policies. Neither the Single European Act nor the Rome conference, however, removed differing national interests or priorities.

Approximately 170 directives designed to implement the EC 1992 program were passed by the Council by the end of 1990. Roughly 130 initiatives remain and pose a real challenge to the EC leadership. Many of the most complicated and contentious drafts have yet to be agreed on by EC bodies. Further, fewer than 25 of those directives passed to member nations for enactment have been approved by all the member countries. The British, perhaps surprisingly given former Prime Minister Margaret Thatcher's influence and rhetoric, have enacted more than any other EC country. The Italians, to date, have not acted on 51 EC-approved directives.

The Commission of the EC is a group of 17 individuals appointed by member nations' governments for four-year terms. As noted, the Commission is responsible for drafting proposals for legislation, which are then submitted for approval, modification or dismissal to the Council of Ministers. If legislation is approved, the Commission is responsible for planning for its implementation on an EC-wide level. Two of the 17 commissioners are German, and the Commission is represented in Bonn by a senior German official.

The European Parliament is the only EC body whose members hold office by winning popularly contested national elections to EC posts. Table 3.4 shows the current party representation in that body. The next elections are scheduled for 1994. The Parliament continues to exercise a basically advisory function with respect to most EC activities, but it does have the authority to reject the EC's annual budget, applications for membership in the EC, and some trade agreements negotiated between the EC and nonmember countries. It can also vote to dismiss the entire Commission, although to date it has not exercised that power. The Parliament can amend legislation; amendments take effect only if they are supported by the Commission and are not vetoed unanimously by the Council.

Efforts to strengthen the Parliament's influence in EC affairs have been somewhat inconsistent. In his Bundestag speech of May 10, 1990, Kohl stated, "If we want European voters to participate in sufficient numbers in the 1994 elections to the European Parliament, we need to give the Parliament more power." German rhetoric in the wake of the December 1990 Rome summit indicates that Chancellor Kohl and Foreign Minister Genscher remain firmly in favor of progress in that direction.

TABLE 3.4
Parties in the European Parliament (Session Ending in 1994)

Party Group[1]	Number of Seats[2]	
Group of the European Right	22	(16)
European Democratic Group (Conservatives)	34	(66)
Liberal and Democratic Reform Group	44	(45)
Group of the European Democratic Alliance	19	(30)
Group of the European People's Party (Christian Democrats)	123	(112)
Nonattached	15	(15)
Socialist Group	181	(166)
Rainbow Group	39	(20)
Communists and Allied Groups	41	(48)

(1) Members are organized by party group, not according to nationality.
(2) Previous totals in parentheses.

Source: *Europe*, July/August 1989, p. 24.

Germany, in cooperation with Belgium, Greece, Italy, and the Netherlands, supports granting Parliament "codecision" powers, meaning that Parliament would have to vote in favor of EC laws or they would not be passed. In the past, the French gave a cool reception to the notion of further strengthening the Parliament. The Kohl-Mitterrand letter of December 1990, however, signaled the French President's symbolic support for the codecision position. The British, once again, are the most likely source of robust opposition. The United Kingdom has reluctantly supported some increases in parliamentary budget control and oversight.

The Parliament would especially like to be granted the right to initiate legislation. The Commission currently holds that power and has strongly opposed all moves that have aimed to give Parliament that capacity.

The 13 judges of the European Court are appointed for six-year terms by the mutual consent of EC member states. The Court is responsible for interpreting the Treaty of Rome and for ruling on member governments' conformity to EC legislation. Its role may increase dramatically should member governments continue to lag in implementing EC directives. Or it could prove to be a bottleneck rather than an impetus to implementation of the 1992 program. Italy and Greece have been most frequently brought before the Court for not implementing EC directives. They are also the nations with the highest backlog of compliance with Court rulings against them.

In contrast, Germany's positive rhetoric roughly corresponds with its demonstrated willingness to pass Community directives into national legislation. It has one of the best records of implementation in the Community. To be sure, controversy over the free movement of legal services, as well as the relatively public squabble over Germany's brewing purity laws, has demonstrated that Germany is not above ignoring Court directives that touch on sensitive national interests. But in the main, such disagreements have been infrequent. In fact, the United Kingdom and Denmark are currently the only nations with better records than Germany with respect to most legislation implemented and fewest derogations from EC directives.

POLITICAL AND ECONOMIC UNION

European Commission President Jacques Delors is the leading advocate of a quick march toward European political and monetary union through a radical restructuring of current EC institutions. But rapid change in the east has caused the EC to direct substantial economic assistance to the former communist nations. This development has led Delors to conclude that the EC's economic policies are too closely linked to political decisions for EC institutions not to have concrete decisionmaking powers in both areas.

A major reason behind his stance for quickly augmenting the role of the EC in monetary and political decisionmaking is his fear that, unless Community institutions have clear powers to act in these areas, some EC members, particularly Germany, might take political initiatives in eastern countries without first consulting through EC channels. Such concern is well placed, especially if the frequently glacial pace of policy initiatives through the EC structure continues to obtain.

European Monetary Union

EC progress on EMU is more advanced than is progress on political union. In December 1990, the Commission reported the results of a survey of EC citizens' opinions on monetary union. Table 3.5 shows the percent of respondents with favorable opinions. The survey also showed that 55 percent of all EC citizens sampled favored a single currency that would replace national currencies in five or six years. Although this approval rate is smaller than the 65 percent or more currently favoring political and security union, the decisionmaking machinery of the EC is farther along the road to making EMU a reality.

Specific proposals for such steps emerged in April 1989, when the Delors committee on monetary union released its report calling for a three-stage progression to a single currency and a single European central bank, Eurofed for short. At the end of 1990, all EC states except the United Kingdom used that three-stage plan as a basis for negotiation.

Stage one began on July 1, 1990. During this initial and ongoing stage, a committee of central bank governors is discussing Community internal monetary policies and external policy coordination. In addition, EC states are being called on to

TABLE 3.5
EC Public Support for EMU

Country	Percent in Favor
Greece	80
Luxembourg	79
Belgium	76
Spain	75
Ireland	74
France	73
Italy	66
Netherlands	56
Germany	51
United Kingdom	37
Denmark	31
Portugal	NA

Source: *Europe*, December 1990, p. 43.

move toward more economic coordination, to free their central banks from direct political control, and to stop printing money to finance their budget deficits.

In the second stage, scheduled to begin on January 1, 1994, Community members will "move toward real convergence." This stage of EMU is currently only slightly elaborated. According to Delors, it is designed to give "those countries not in a position to enter EMU immediately the time to catch up with the rest of the Community." Stage two is also designed as a period in which the Eurofed could consolidate its power and independence.

The January 1, 1994 starting date for stage two was set by Chancellor Kohl and 10 other EC members at an EC summit in October 1990 in spite of British opposition. Many interpreted that German action as an indication of political support for a relatively fast track toward EMU. But in the last days of 1990, German public pronouncements emphasized that a starting date for stage two would be of little importance if persistent economic divergences among EC nations still existed at the start of January 1994. This evident shift toward the Bundesbank's public position on EMU portends two developments that could be termed important. First, substantial German public opposition could develop in the face of any moves toward EMU that might appear to sacrifice Germany's traditional strong anti-inflation stance. Second, the Germans are resisting vocal French pressure to move quickly on EMU and are displaying a new public independence within EC circles.

Some EC planners believe that preparations for the move to stage three might begin as early as 1997. Although this schedule is theoretically possible, it would require enormous political and economic discipline and convergence. In this final stage, the Eurofed would control EC-wide monetary policy. The Community would have a single currency.

In contrast, the United Kingdom has, since summer 1990, pursued a program aimed at producing a "hard ECU." Prime Minister John Major, the initial and principal advocate of the hard ECU plan in Thatcher's last government, has stated that any rapid moves toward a single EC currency would create "intolerable" strains that could divide the Community along lines of relative prosperity.

The position of the Bundesbank, the German central bank, on monetary union has been conservative. The deutsche mark continues to be the strongest currency in Europe, and the decline of the dollar only accentuates the DM's role as a global reserve currency. Concerns exist in some German quarters about a potential weakening of the DM should inflation increase as a result of east German reforms. But the Bundesbank takes pride in its record of keeping inflation levels down.

The Bundesbank currently advocates a cautious movement toward European economic union. Its directors believe that the extent to which member states achieve monetary stability should be the key factor in determining the pace of EMU. Its position is that many EC members will have to restructure their economies fundamentally to make such a union viable. Many German bankers do not believe that all EC members will exercise monetary and fiscal restraint to the extent that Germany has. The Bundesbank will, therefore, probably not support the creation of EMU without strong guarantees of the independence of a central bank. It has not publicly supported Kohl's advocacy of the January 1, 1994 deadline for the start of stage two of EMU. Kohl's rhetoric at the end of 1990 suggested that he was moving closer to the Bundesbank and Finance Ministry position that demonstrable economic convergence and a truly independent Eurofed are necessary conditions for German support of stages two and three.

Karl Otto Poehl, President of the Bundesbank, has expressed reservations concerning the willingness of some member governments and parliaments to transfer sovereign rights to a European central bank. He believes that it is vital for such a bank to have the same degree of independence and flexibility as the Bundesbank. He speaks for many Germans who are unwilling to give up the stability and dependability of the DM until the Community can guarantee that its replacement will be at least as good.

> "He who wants Europe's success must pursue a policy of political and economic stability; the most important pillar is monetary stability."
>
> Tyll Necker, President of the Federation of German Industries

The French may be predisposed to grant Poehl's wishes. In the 1980s, under the European Monetary System (EMS), France lost a great deal of influence over its economy to Bundesbank directors. Tension between France and Germany arose in late 1990 over the issue of monetary cooperation. France argued that the growing German budget deficit had kept interest rates artificially high at a time when France would have liked to ease its monetary policy. Jacques de Larosière, Governor of the Bank of France, warned that the EMS was reaching its limits for monetary cooperation. He is by no means alone in France in his belief that the EC should make the most rapid progress possible toward EMU. The core of his support rests on the fact that EMU would likely reduce German influence in EC monetary decisions.

A significant number of Germans have expressed reservations about the relative security of a common European currency in comparison with the record of the DM. Stability of the DM is very important psychologically to many Germans. In 1990, German political leaders deliberately chose to push ahead on EMU faster than the Bundesbank counseled. This policy emphasized Germany's commitment to Europeanism. But Kohl has been careful to limit endorsement of the Eurofed concept. His desire is for a body free from political influence and as committed to price stability as is the present Bundesbank. He has also been careful to make clear that he expects French support for a relatively fast track toward political union and more clearly democratic Community institutions.

In the final statement of the EC Council's December 1990 Rome summit, members agreed to move toward stage two of EMU. However, some signs of fractionation over the eventual requirements of that stage are already emerging. German Finance Minister Theo Waigel, in particular, has suggested that if the Community cannot agree on what constitutes adequate budgetary discipline for the start of stage two, the EC should merely strengthen the EC Central Bank Governors' Committee instead of establishing the Eurofed. The Dutch have advanced similar suggestions. The Spanish have been somewhat open to the British proposal for a hard ECU to be the central step in stage two. Continued French insistence on political accountability for the Eurofed could put them on a collision course with the Germans, who, as noted above, regard the independence of a central bank as a necessary condition for successful monetary policy.

Clearly, the implementation of stage two poses substantial difficulties. The Community risks splitting those nations willing and able to meet German ideals for economic convergence from those who cannot or will not.

The popular will to move toward some form of EMU is apparently substantial. As recession threatens and growth rates slow, however, the pain of making tough economic decisions in the march toward economic discipline may at times be acute. Political leaders face dire electoral consequences if their constituents' pain associated with monetary union is severe.

In the process of regularizing German currency, a certain tolerance for economic pain has developed on both sides of the Elbe. If the Germans lead the Europeans in the direction of a common currency, they run the risk of creating further discomfort outside their own borders in populations that will be ill-inclined to suffer through economic discipline. The electoral consequences for political leaders in EC member states associated with decisions on common currency may well prove to be intolerable. In short, there is no easy course to monetary union. In fact, German leadership in that direction may turn out to be widely resented.

There would seem to be little question about German willingness to lead in economic matters. In spite of the challenges of unification, few analysts dispute German capabilities in that respect. But it will take substantial diplomatic sensitivity and skill to dampen resentment of what soon must be recognized as German economic pre-eminence, if not dominance, within Europe and accompanying German freedom of action in the global economy.

Political Union

It would be a mistake, however, to regard monetary union as a stalking horse for political union. Although most EC states theoretically support the goal of monetary union and a single European currency, there is little agreement among EC members on timetables and mechanisms in the currency realm, to say nothing of common political goals. The tensions made evident in early 1991 by the war in the Persian Gulf illustrate just how different security and foreign policy concerns can be from technical economic deliberations.

This is true in part because discussions on EMU have been taking place for a longer time; in part because it is easier to identify necessary and sufficient steps toward EMU than to identify parallel political steps; and in part because member states' positions on delegating sovereign political authority are much more split than are the same states' comparative positions on EMU. This state of affairs was well documented by the diverging foreign policy positions of EC member countries concerning the war in the Persian Gulf.

The Single European Act enables many Council decisions to be decided on a majority, rather than a unanimous, basis. Traditionally, "democracy" in EC decisions was justified by the theory that member state parliaments exercise direct control over the national leaders, who are Council members, and voters exercise direct control over the members of parliaments. Thus, a national parliament could ensure that no EC legislation to which it was opposed passed in spite of its opposition. Although the use of majority voting in some areas has greatly sped the progress of the 1992 program, it has also raised "tyranny of the majority" questions. Potentially, decisions could be reached in the face of overt hostility from a Council member.

The clear benefits of a unified Community political policy have led many in the EC to support steps toward European political unity. Foreign and security policies are and have traditionally been outside the purview of Community deliberations, but as subsequent discussion of European security will suggest, they may not remain there.

The clear losses of national sovereignty associated with such moves have led some members vehemently to oppose them. Political fine tuning will continue as the Inter-governmental Conference on political union progresses. But real political union will await further deepening of Community political structures—perhaps through a gradual strengthening of the European Parliament—as well as further deepening of Community economic ties.

Mitterrand has argued that EMU is much easier to define than is political union. Certainly, the plans for political union are quite vague and mainly aimed at increasing the number of policy areas where the EC has a mandate to speak for the Community. The leaders at the Rome summit authorized the formation of an IGC on political unity that is to consider the effect of extending EC authority over a number of areas. Negotiators at this conference are to appraise various general suggestions for changing the Treaty of Rome, including proposals to:

- strengthen the European Parliament;

- create a European citizenship;

- completely drop any unanimity rules that still obtain in Council meetings; and

- turn over to Community bodies the authority to regulate policies regarding the environment, basic research, immigration, visas, drug interdiction and organized crime, and to develop and supervise some additional international social programs.

Each of these moves can be seen to strengthen Germany's already powerful stance in a new Europe. Unified Germany's large population makes a strong case for increased German representation in Parliament and hence its influence there. In fact, anticipation of this problem has already ruffled diplomatic feathers in France, Italy and the United Kingdom, each of which currently has the same number of European parliamentarians as does Germany. German leadership in environmental matters and basic research is already acknowledged. Similar German leadership on the other topics is likely to develop for reasons of Germany's size and location, and especially because of the exigencies of unification.

NEW EC MEMBERS?

Sentiment in the EC is largely against expanding membership in the Community until after the 1992 program is implemented. This state of affairs will provide Germany with some breathing space; but all too soon Germany will have to reconcile its policies toward the west with imperatives arising in the east.

Germany has consistently supported initiatives to deepen the Community. Kohl has repeatedly emphasized the need to legitimize the Community by granting more power to

"It would be wrong to attempt to integrate as many countries as possible into the EC. The Community would not survive such an effort without damage. If we want European unity, we must limit membership for the time being to those countries which are willing and able to create such unity."

Chancellor Kohl, October 1990

the European Parliament. Bonn has emphasized the importance of strengthening Community institutions before new members are admitted. Still, many German politicians remain convinced that increasing political cooperation and delegation of sovereignty to Community bodies does not rule out extending EC membership to other European nations. German officials have also supported concluding association agreements with the eastern European countries as soon as possible, which, in practical terms, probably means after the January 1, 1993 deadline for completion of the internal market. German policymakers welcome the time to plan for orderly accession of eastern European states.

> *"During the coming years, it will be our task to enhance the political and economic partnership with our European neighbors in the east. We do not want to limit Europe to the Community of Twelve; we believe that everybody should participate like us to overcome the division of Europe."*
>
> Chancellor Kohl,
> State of the Union Address, 1990

In addition to eastern European countries seeking to join the EC, numerous western European nations and one southern European nation are also candidates for membership. Turkey already has association agreements with the EC and is likely to seek German support for full membership given the large Turkish population there. Austria has announced its intention to apply for membership. Sweden's Parliament has voted in favor of making an application. Norway, Iceland, Finland, and Switzerland are other likely applicants.

The European Free Trade Association (EFTA) (see Appendix 1) is currently negotiating with the EC on the formation of a European Economic Area (EEA) that is aimed at liberalizing the flow of goods, services, capital, and labor among member states of both organizations by the beginning of 1993. However, the negotiating parties disagree even over the name of the area. This perhaps foreshadows the eventual outcome of negotiations.

Germany is a natural advocate of policies that will help to ensure economic and political stability on its eastern borders. Unnecessarily interventionist German policies, however, may well offend even those neighbors who may be nominal beneficiaries of such policies. Extension of associate or full membership in the EC to include eastern European nations could serve to lend international legitimacy to policies Germany favors.

In the near term, Germany will continue to support deepening measures that will reassure its present partners as well as provide economic and political benefits for itself. Such policies will likely help to reassure neighbors that German unification will be a controlled process taking place within a strictly western European context.

It was in such a limited, western European context that Germany's post-World War II reputation for monetary prudence, fiscal stability and political deference was made. That reputation needs protection if Germany's inevitable emergence as a leader in eastern European affairs is to be viewed by Europe and the world as beneficent and benign.

OPPORTUNITY COSTS OF UNIFICATION

A number of analysts in Germany, the European Community and the United States have stated publicly their reservations about the costs to Germany's economic partners of financing unification. Some EC Commission members worry that in the absence of higher EC saving rates, financing unification will intensify the scarcity of capital in Europe and thus support continued high interest rates there. As estimates of German public sector deficits have risen, some of Germany's partners have wondered whether the strains of unification might endanger Germany's rock-solid monetary record. The Bundesbank has taken steps to ensure that its reputation, its low inflation rate and its currency do not suffer. However, the strong FDP showing in the December 1990 German election did little to allay these concerns outside Germany. The FDP supports making eastern Germany a low tax zone.

THE EC BUDGET

West Germany has been a principal contributor of funds to support weaker members of the EC. Many of Germany's EC partners fear that the fiscal pressures of unification as well as the addition of a large, poorer area to Germany may serve to reduce the amount Germany contributes to such EC institutions as the structural funds program. Through that program, relatively rich EC nations provide economic assistance to relatively poor EC nations. Poor countries worry that this might presage lower levels of support for them. Richer countries worry that they might be asked to pay more as Germany rebuilds its eastern states.

Policy decisions in Bonn on these matters are politically volatile. West German taxpayers are nervous about the cost to them associated with east German reconstruction. Indeed, taxpayers throughout Germany may well become highly self-interested with regard to near-term distribution of economic support outside Germany. EC members will be observant as well as cautious and perhaps hostile should economic myopia in Germany reduce available benefits accruing to poorer countries within the Community.

FINANCING UNIFICATION

It is not only Germany's fellow EC members that are concerned with the external effects of financing German unification. Business, financial and some political leaders in the United States also worry about the effects unification will have on German foreign investment and on international interest rates if modernization efforts are financed primarily through borrowing rather than through tax revenues. Outsiders tend to worry when German bankers shrug their shoulders in reply to questions about unification costs or reply that the issue of cost is quite irrelevant. But no informed analyst doubts that Germany will spend whatever is necessary to ensure the stability and prosperity of its eastern states.

More than one German policymaker has described and by implication defended the course currently being taken by the Kohl government in the following way:

- Regardless of the cost, substantial infrastructure investment must be made in eastern Germany.

- However, the amount that can be invested in a particular year is limited by a number of factors, including structural economic reform, availability of trained personnel and lack of communications infrastructure.

- Therefore, the rebuilding process will take longer than some in Germany might consider desirable.

- However, capacity constraints that limit annual investment will make financing investment easier.

- Some costs of unification will be financed through the disposal of state property or through private investment in eastern Germany.

- Further, Germany's public sector deficits in 1990 and 1991 may be high in comparison with recent FRG deficits, but they are not inconsistent with those of some other industrialized nations.

- Therefore, undue strain will not be placed on international capital markets.

In summary, proponents of this line conclude that investment in and support for eastern Germany will proceed without serious long-term implications for the international capital markets. They also assert that current DM interest rates are artificially high and are likely to fall.

There are, however, two important unstated assumptions on which these arguments are based. The first is that Germany will not "run out of money" to finance unification. The second is that in the near term the overall costs of unification are unimportant to the parties concerned with financing that process.

Politically speaking, the consequences for western Germany of unrestrained migration from or widespread insurrection in the east make the first assumption necessary. The second is defensible only if political fiat dampens competition for development capital originating outside Germany.

This circular and definitely optimistic argument reflects concerns of German policymakers trying to manage the revitalization of the east and of many in Germany involved in financing that process. However, the argument does gainsay the concerns of many analysts trying to understand how financing German unification will affect global financial markets.

CURRENT DEMANDS FOR CAPITAL

German unification is clearly not the only cause of increasing international demand for capital. The continuing, though slowing, economic growth rates in the industrial world fuel an enormous amount of investment activity. On the one hand, such investment is not extraordinary. On the other hand, many substantial investment projects under way or about to begin could hardly have been foreseen only a few years ago.

The liberalization of central Europe and the drive toward developing market economies there have created an enormous demand for investment capital that will increase as the countries of eastern Europe develop. The substantial rise in the cost of oil and Soviet insistence on hard currency in return for energy shipments are forcing eastern Europeans to borrow from the west when they already have difficulty servicing their existing hard currency debt. The eastern European regimes need more capital to satisfy political expectations in the wake of communism's demise. But their financial position requires not only tolerance and patience but also significant debt forgiveness or rescheduling and further support.

Meanwhile, the EC 1992 program has prompted significant investment increases within the EC by European and foreign firms and investors. According to the Commission, should

TABLE 3.6
U.S. Federal Government Deficit and U.S. GDP, 1980-90
($ Billion)

	1980	1981	1982	1983	1984	1985	1986	1987	1988	1989	1990
GDP	2,684	3,001	3,115	3,356	3,725	3,974	4,205	4,497	4,840	5,163	5,416P
Fed. gov. deficit	−76	−79	−216	−203	−178	−212	−213	−147	−156	−142P	−92f
% of GDP	2.8	2.6	4.0	6.0	4.8	5.3	5.1	3.3	3.2	2.8	

(p) Provisional.
(f) First half of year only, provisional.

Source: International Financial Statistics, IMF.

Europe prove relatively recession-proof in comparison with the United States, capital investment needs of firms in the EC are expected to double in the next decade.

The U.S. budget deficit (see Table 3.6) is likely to remain high, in part because of the cost of maintaining forces in the Persian Gulf during the 1991 war. According to International Monetary Fund (IMF) figures, more than 40 percent of that deficit is financed by foreign money from the EC. It is not just a potential decrease in German direct investment in the United States that worries some U.S. public and private leaders. If less

German capital flows to other EC nations, they in turn may invest less in the United States, particularly if U.S. interest rates remain relatively low. Adding together all these demands for capital suggests that the world's largest debtor nation may be competing (possibly successfully) for capital sorely needed to rebuild eastern Germany and eastern Europe.

FOREIGN INVESTMENT IN AMERICA

In 1990, the U.S. dollar lost considerable value compared with other currencies. It depreciated nearly 10 percent against the DM in the first 10 months of 1990, reaching the lowest comparative level since the end of World War II. The United States has a relatively high inflation rate compared with Germany and a decreasing rate of economic growth. Such figures may, as one German banker put it, "lead foreign investors to conclude that investing in the U.S. is simply a poor investment decision when compared with investing within the EC."

Additional disincentives to foreign investors are the Federal Reserve Bank's December 1990 cut in the discount rate from 7.0 to 6.5 percent and its January 1991 further cut to 6.0 percent. These moves were made in part because the U.S. central bank feared a credit crunch that could restrict the availability of U.S. investment capital even to healthy firms there. Repeatedly weak major economic indicators, such as employment statistics and industrial production levels, also served to convince the Fed that interest rates could be lowered without damaging the economy by reversing the downward trend in inflation.

> "I think we have to deal with a very difficult set of economic problems in this country. We have 4 percent real interest rates right now and about 1 percent economic growth. That's a corrosive environment for any capital-intensive business."
>
> Leading U.S. banker,
> Fall 1990

Lower interest rates mean that the dollar's position may well slide further. A combination of the dollar's sinking value compared with the deutsche mark, the relatively high though declining inflation rate in the United States, and the relatively low U.S. rates of interest and economic growth may tend to discourage foreign investment in America. Alternatively, the United States will need to raise interest rates to attract foreign capital.

GERMAN INVESTMENT

Within 24 hours of the Fed's December 1990 announcement, *The Monthly Report of the Deutsche Bundesbank* was released, noting that German interest rates would be raised if the government's indebtedness threatened the "controlled expansion of credit and the money supply." This statement was realized at the end of January when the Bundesbank raised both the discount and the Lombard rates (see Table 3.7 for German interest rates through January 1991). This move reflected a long-standing concern of the bank's directors that net German public borrowing to finance unification rose significantly in 1990. According to Bundesbank figures, net borrowing in the market by central, regional and local authorities in the second quarter of 1990 was almost three times higher than it was in the same quarter of 1989—DM 21.6 billion as opposed to DM 7.8 billion.

"But if Germany, now playing an even more critical role in world capital markets, runs large budget deficits to finance its investments in eastern Germany, U.S. interest rates could be driven up by as much as a half a percentage point in 1991, and a full point in 1992 through 1995."

Lee H. Hamilton, Chairman, Joint Economic Committee, U.S. Congress

The Bundesbank fears that a combination of near-term unification costs, low tax revenues in the former GDR and recently reduced tax rates in western Germany will lead the public sector to borrow extremely heavily in the credit markets. The GDR collected taxes totaling only DM 1 billion in July and about DM 2.5 billion in August 1990. According to the Ministry of Finance, this was approximately 14 percent of the expected revenue cited in the GDR budget for the second half of the year.

In addition, the argument goes, a larger share of European capital is likely to be invested in European projects, while a larger share of German money is likely to be invested in Germany. The Bundesbank remarked in its September 1990 *Monthly Report* that Germans invested directly abroad at a sig-

TABLE 3.7
German Interest Rates

Applicable From:			Discount % p.a.*	Lombard % p.a.*
1980	Feb	29	7.0	8.5
	May	2	7.5	9.5
	Sep	19	7.5	9.0
1982	Aug	27	7.0	8.0
	Oct	22	7.0	7.0
	Dec	3	5.0	6.0
1983	Mar	18	4.0	5.0
	Sep	9	4.0	5.5
1984	Jun	29	4.5	5.5
1985	Feb	1	4.5	6.0
	Aug	16	4.0	5.5
1986	Mar	7	3.5	5.5
1987	Jan	23	3.0	5.0
	Nov	6	3.0	4.5
	Dec	4	2.5	4.5
1988	Jul	1	3.0	4.5
	Jul	29	3.0	5.0
	Aug	26	3.5	5.0
	Dec	16	3.5	5.5
1989	Jan	20	4.0	6.0
	Apr	21	4.5	6.5
	Jun	30	5.0	7.0
	Oct	6	6.0	8.0
1990	Nov	2	6.0	8.5
1991	Jan	31	6.5	9.0

* Per annum.

Sources: *The Monthly Report of the Deutsche Bundesbank* and The *Financial Times*.

nificantly lower rate in the second quarter of 1990 (DM 21.5 billion) than they did in the first quarter (DM 38.0 billion). However, the rate of foreign investment in Germany more than doubled in the second quarter of 1990 compared with the level at the beginning of 1990. In addition, the bank noted, "German enterprises invested about 30 percent less capital in foreign branches and subsidiaries or in the purchase of foreign participating interests in the second quarter than in the first, when direct investment reached the record level of DM 9.5 billion."

This figure is of particular concern to the United States, because in 1989 it was the most important country of destination for German direct investment. German direct investment in the United States fell dramatically in the first half of 1990.

What should this flux mean to concerned parties in the United States? The U.S. public demand for foreign capital is not decreasing. American interest rates are dropping. The U.S. savings rate shows no signs of significant increases.

The German public and private demand for capital is rising both because of reconstruction in the east and because of sustained economic growth in the west. German interest rates remain high. German savings rates have not risen substantially. German public expenditure is increasing dramatically. Foreign investment in Germany, in other EC nations and in eastern Europe is also increasing.

Put bluntly, there is no way to be sure how these factors will affect the cost of capital and the level of investment in the

> *"You can see the claims on capital in the world everywhere you look. The Germans are in the process of financing the integration of their nation, and I think, from a human point of view, that is one of the more welcome integrations that we've seen because it has been accomplished peacefully. But it's putting calls on capital.*
>
> *Interest rates are going to be very high. Traditionally, economic integration is financed with inflation. The Germans are trying to do it without inflation. If they do, they're going to have to ration capital and cut back on consumption to make room for more investment and more savings."*
>
> John Reed, Chairman, Citicorp,
> October 1990

United States. But continued high German interest rates and spending could create tension between Germany and the United States should the recession in the United States deepen.

TRADE ISSUES

Particularly given the setbacks in the GATT Uruguay Round, Germany risks appearing to many in America as the leader of a bloc that is becoming dangerously shortsighted in trade matters. Meanwhile, the European Community as a whole has raised U.S. hackles for stubbornness that crippled recent GATT talks on agricultural subsidies. The EC and American refusals to modify their respective positions on agricultural trade issues have lost both parties a substantial degree of respect in other nations. Both parties have taken first steps down dangerously self-righteous paths.

Accusations of protectionism and dumping continue to be traded between the EC and America on this issue. It remains to be seen if EC discussions of CAP supports will lead to concessions that might allow talks to resume. Some Americans had hoped that Germany would soften its support for the EC agricultural position after the December 1990 election. However, Chancellor Kohl has made clear his belief that Germany does not have a responsibility to change this Community policy.

However, export growth is a bright sign for American manufacturers. The National Association of Manufacturers predicts that export growth will be about 25 percent between 1990 and 1993. But it is worth remembering that exports account for only about 13 percent of U.S. GDP. Thus, even significant export growth would probably be insufficient to reverse a substantial recession. Still, export sales could help soften the downturn. In addition, although the U.S. trade deficit with Asian nations has broadened in recent years, the deficit with Europe has dropped.

But this progress is threatened by the present impasse in the GATT negotiations. There is more than enough blame for all parties. The U.S. position on trade in services has led to charges that it is preserving its rights to unilateral action in sensitive areas such as express mail, parcel shipping and air transport. The problem is that while America would like to preserve its ability to pry open markets by allocating concessions on a bilateral basis, the GATT agreement operates on a most-favored-nation principle. That approach, which means that what is opened to one trading partner should in principle be opened to all, has caused U.S. trade officials and members of Congress to express concern over the extent of government support for business, not only in Japan but in Europe in general and in Germany in particular.

OUTLOOK

In 1986, 1987 and 1988, west Germany exported more goods than any other country in the world. In 1989, the United States regained its previous, long-standing lead position.

Western Germany exports approximately 35 percent of its GNP. Its current account surplus in 1989 was almost at the level of Japan's—more than $55 billion. Germany is an integral part of the world economy and has a stake in its growth, stability and liberalization. Other trading states have a vested interest in Germany's growth, stability and liberalization.

Many private sector observers have warned that the lack of progress in the GATT round will have serious effects on the growth of international trade. The international trading system risks becoming a system of negative rather than positive reinforcement. Since the formation of the GATT, a major incentive for countries to open their markets has been the willingness of other nations, especially the United States, to lead the way toward liberalization. This trend may reverse if both the United States and the EC, with Germany leading or following, decide that the way to open markets abroad is temporarily to refuse access to their own domestic markets.

One sign of the growth of such sentiment in America is the support of a vocal minority of policymakers for reciprocity in trade relations. These advocates of greater government interference in trade often support bilateral rather than multilateral agreements, arguing that they increase U.S. leverage and minimize trade openings to nations that do not reciprocate.

Traditionally, the United States has supported the concept of national treatment of foreign firms. In other words, any foreign corporation operating in the United States is treated according to the same rules that apply to similar U.S. corporations. In return, the United States expects that U.S. firms will be subject in foreign countries to the same rules that govern a host country's domestic corporations in the same sector.

Indeed, U.S. negotiators fought hard against EC rules applying reciprocal measures in the financial services industry.

The U.S. government position is that fairness is much easier to achieve through national treatment than through complicated bilateral reciprocal agreements. In addition, U.S. policymakers often point out that it may not be in the U.S. interest to adopt the same treatment in all sectors. Public support in some sectors for a more restrictive neomercantilist concept of reciprocity in trade is becoming noticeable.

These concerns are real, but in general, German influence in economic affairs within and outside Europe has created little

TABLE 3.8
U.S.-German Trade, 1986-89
(U.S.$ Million)

	1986	1987	1988	1989
Exports to the U.S. from Germany	25,519	27,877	26,020	24,835
Exports to Germany from the U.S.	10,561	11,748	14,269	16,883
German surplus	14,958	16,129	11,751	7,952

Source: Derived from *Direction of Trade Statistics Yearbook 1990*, IMF.

friction between Washington and Bonn. Nervousness in Paris, London and elsewhere has been more intense than in New York or Washington. But sustained German growth based on successful incorporation of its eastern states may lead to increased anxiety among American policymakers about German domination of the European economy post-1992.

The German position as first among its EC fellows is a major consideration in the future of relations between the United States and Germany in particular and the United States and the European Community in general. It is instructive to note that Germany's gross exports to the United States have substantially exceeded U.S. gross exports to Germany. Still, as can be seen in Table 3.8, the relative deficit is diminishing.

This state of affairs underlines a basic tension that could emerge between Germany, a state extremely dependent on foreign trade, and the United States, a state with continuing substantial foreign trade and current account deficits. U.S. proposals to increase taxes on luxury items, like automobiles, concern Germans who view themselves as potentially vulnerable targets of the policies. Differences between the two nations on agricultural issues, COCOM regulations and services industry issues, among others, help ensure that trade will remain an area with a high potential for misunderstanding and conflict.

An impasse on the GATT may also increase strains between the executive branch in the United States and the Congress, and endanger U.S.-European and U.S.-German cooperation in other areas such as security. As one U.S. senator suggested, it is much easier to count tanks and missiles than to evaluate dollar losses in reduced trade. Irritation over complicated sectoral disagreements could be manifested in security policy as Congress wields much more effective influence on security issues than on the less organized and more complicated economic issues. Thus, general levels of resentment in Congress over European actions could extend from trade into other areas.

Economic tensions between the EC and the United States are rising at the same time as the transatlantic security structure is being reassessed. Cooperation and understanding between Europe and America on security issues will be essential if the global interests of both are to be served. Developing a new security system for the west will be difficult. Patience, diligence and forbearance will be called for as members of the North Atlantic Treaty Organization, the Western European Union, the European Community, and the Conference on Security and Cooperation in Europe reassess institutional arrangements. Germany and the United States occupy central positions in those developments.

CHAPTER FOUR

Security for Unified Germany

Germans today enjoy a standard of living and a quality of life unlikely to have been envisioned even by the most convinced optimists at the end of World War II. The postwar period provided an opportunity for Germany under the Marshall Plan and the NATO umbrella to recover from the devastation of war and build an economy that is the envy of its neighbors and the base not only for unification but also for German leadership within Europe. The security structure within which the Federal Republic grew allowed comity to prevail in the west while strong deterrents were created to any military ventures from the east.

That security structure is now being seriously re-examined. The end of Soviet hegemony in eastern Europe and the remarkable decay of the communist system within the Soviet Union have removed a clearly identifiable threat around which members of the North Atlantic alliance coalesced for four decades.

Newly unified Germany finds itself at the center of an unfamiliar and challenging security situation. The stability provided by counterbalancing alliances no longer exists, and the course of developments in the Soviet Union remains uncertain.

German leaders have been quick to emphasize their determination to remain firmly anchored in the western alliance system. But that system is changing, and Germany's role in it is
bound to shift as a result of the leadership position Germany
has acquired. The capacity of Germany's east European neighbors to deal with the monumental problems of democratization
and transformation into capitalist economies is far from guaranteed. Moreover, the Germans face a residue of Soviet-induced
difficulties within what are now their own borders.

These security considerations have political, diplomatic and
economic as well as defense-related significance. German security involves, among other factors, the ability to establish and
maintain friendly relations with its neighbors, to manifest its
desire for economic development and stability along its borders,
to deal with problems of differential economic growth and related immigration, and to maintain the military forces necessary
to deal with significant threats to security that might emerge.

Development of a security regime that protects German
interests will take place within the context of the economic
organizations previously discussed. Indeed, the end product of
many economic arrangements in which Germany is presently
involved will include a security regime that is truly European,
but with unified Germany as its strongest and central single
state. Lenin's dictum that the road to Europe lies through
Berlin has acquired new relevance.

Germany's freedom of action in international affairs has
increased dramatically in the past year. How the Germans deal
with their shifting security environment is a major factor in the
foreign policy calculations of leaders in Washington and Moscow
as well as throughout Europe.

Germans have shown a marked tendency to remember history and to take account of their neighbors' sensibilities. But
Germany is now in a position of leadership at a time of great
uncertainty. Its security concerns extend far beyond the military.

In spite of changes in Soviet policy, the most likely threat to
Germany lies in the east, where the demise of communism has
created great economic expectations unlikely to be met easily or
soon. Simultaneously, Germany has committed to remain a key
player in western organizations that are themselves changing.
Further, the residue of Soviet influence in eastern Germany is
cause for continuing concern.

CHANGES IN THE EAST

The most dramatic changes in the German security environment are occurring in the east. Gorbachev's moves toward substantial reduction in Soviet troop strength and his decision to withdraw troops from the Warsaw Pact countries have been major sources of encouragement for those who wish to end communist domination in eastern Germany and to unify the states of the GDR with the Federal Republic. Gorbachev's initiatives, whether motivated by a desire to reduce tensions, by a desire to reduce costs, or both, set the stage for the remarkable events occurring between the destruction of the Berlin Wall in November 1989 and elections in a unified Germany in December 1990.

The drawdown in Soviet troop strength and weaponry in eastern Europe affects a broader range of concerns than just those of Germany. The erosion of stringent Soviet control of Warsaw Pact nations, the abandonment of the Brezhnev Doctrine, the discreditation of Marxist-Leninist ideology in eastern Europe, and the move toward market economies combined to create an environment in which Germany could achieve unification. Perhaps most important, Gorbachev's decision to allow united Germany to become NATO's strongest European member dramatically emphasized changing power realities in Europe.

Those decisions by the Soviet leader involved political and other costs that have yet to run their course. For this and other reasons, a number of dangers are built into the new situation in the Soviet Union and Germany. The Soviet army has been less than enthusiastic about the reduced priority it is receiving under *perestroika*. Soviet troops in eastern Germany are not due to be removed entirely until the end of 1994, and this could be a source of further friction and instability. The morale of Soviet soldiers in Germany is reportedly extremely poor, and discipline is suffering.

The situation is complicated by the overt hostility of the Germans toward their "guests." Further resentment stems from Germany's agreement to pay for the withdrawal of 600,000 Soviet troops from the Warsaw Pact countries. In spite of the German willingness to pay dearly, no evidence exists that Gorbachev is accelerating withdrawal of these troops, perhaps because most of them, when released from service in the Soviet Union, will create pressures in the USSR as they search for housing and jobs. Table 4.1 shows the number of Soviet as well as other foreign troops in united Germany.

TABLE 4.1
Foreign Troops in Germany, 1990

U.S.	244,200	Soviet Union	370,000
U.K.	67,200		
France	52,700		
Belgium	24,900		
Canada	7,100		
Netherlands	5,700		

Note: Figures are estimates for fall 1990. NATO forces formally garrisoned in Germany but deployed to the Persian Gulf are included.

Sources: International Institute for Strategic Studies, U.S. Department of Defense, and German Ministry of Defense.

In spite of the slow pace of withdrawal, the capacity of the Soviet Union to engage in a successful military adventure at this time is highly circumscribed. Soviet leaders could resort to nuclear threats or nuclear employment, but that eventuality is not likely.

As a result, Germany, like most of its allies, is seriously considering significant reductions in troop levels. Indeed, prior to unification, Chancellor Kohl announced that the German armed forces would draw down from roughly 470,000 to 370,000 military personnel. That decision was reconfirmed at the end of 1990.

The GDR army has, for all practical purposes, disintegrated. Although officers and some cadre remain in uniform in caretaker status, the military effectiveness of the organization is near zero. Unresolved, politically sensitive questions include whether to incorporate members of the GDR army into the Bundeswehr, how many officers and personnel should be allowed to join and what retraining would be required. By and large, present efforts are directed toward placing former east German military personnel in jobs in the civilian sector. Most of the equipment previously held by east German forces has been taken under Bundeswehr control, and some equipment, including a number of tanks, has been destroyed.

None of the foregoing should obscure the point that the Soviet Union remains a major military power both in terms of its conventional capabilities and in terms of its possession of nuclear weapons (see Table 4.2). The threat that Soviet forces

TABLE 4.2
Soviet Armed Forces, 1990

Total Active Personnel: 4,000,000* Reserves (to Age 50): 5,600,000

Ground Forces		Air Forces	
Motorized rifle divisions	127	Bombers	700
Tank divisions	45	Attack aircraft	4,000
Airborne divisions	7	Interceptors	2,000
Static defense divisions	3	Antiair missiles	8,000
		Naval aircraft	1,200
Naval Forces		Land-based ballistic	
Aircraft carriers	4	missiles	1,500
Guided missile cruisers	2	Submarine-launched	
Principal surface		ballistic missiles	950
combatants	105		
Frigates and corvettes	121		
Minesweepers	105		
Patrol boats	120		
Amphibious warfare ships	82		
Ballistic missile			
submarines	63		
Attack submarines	61		
Other submarines	31		

* All figures are rounded.

Sources: IISS (London) and U.S. Department of Defense.

pose to emerging eastern European democracies is every bit as much a concern to Germany as is the threat that those forces might pose to western Europe.

Moreover, the Soviet military is a significant political force in Moscow. Many of the adjustments that Gorbachev made in the structure of the Soviet government in late 1990 reflected his concern that the Soviet military and intelligence services continue to worry about erosion of their own relative power positions under *perestroika.*

Beyond these considerations, Germans have little reason to look to national military forces in Poland, Czechoslovakia or Hungary as buffers against possible Soviet military moves. The future of those forces remains uncertain for a variety of reasons, including lack of money, weakening of ideological motivation, and erosion of whatever cohesive effects Soviet "leadership" may have provided.

Change in the Soviet Union and the disappearance of military confrontation in eastern Europe have not eliminated German security concerns. Instability within the Soviet Union or, worse, the re-emergence of a xenophobic authoritarian regime are possibilities that German policymakers cannot ignore. Insurance in the form of German military forces is expensive but essential in the eyes of policymakers in Bonn and in allied capitals.

Diplomatic contact between Bonn and Moscow, so carefully nurtured through *Ostpolitik*, remains critical. Some analysts argue that the USSR is effectively blackmailing Germany for hard currency in exchange for withdrawing Soviet troops from eastern Germany and eastern Europe. Soviet nuclear systems still threaten German targets. Soviet internal unrest is a matter of grave concern, especially if it should spill over into eastern Europe.

There are, however, sound reasons on both sides for maintaining good relations. Extension of the Soviet-German dialogue, both bilaterally and within the Conference on Security and Cooperation in Europe (CSCE), is a high priority within the German Foreign Ministry and a central element in the German search for security.

POLITICAL AND ECONOMIC CONSIDERATIONS

Germany's strong interest in political and economic progress in the Soviet Union is not, of course, driven by security factors alone. Germany and the Soviet Union could become significant business partners, especially in the trade of Soviet raw materials for German know-how and products. And, although Germans and Russians have battled each other repeatedly over the centuries, Germans have not forgotten that the final decision on unification came as a result of a meeting between Chancellor Kohl and President Gorbachev at which no third party was present.

In the long run, thoughtful German leaders and analysts recognize the necessity to provide an opportunity for a reorganized and reoriented Soviet Union or its successor state to enter Europe as an equal partner. In fact, many Germans are eager to see that this development takes place as quickly as possible.

Soviet political disarray and economic difficulties are undesirable not only in humanitarian terms. They provide tremendous practical difficulties for Poland, Czechoslovakia and Hungary and, by extension, for Germany. Already, shortages of fuel and food in the USSR are causing officials in Prague and Budapest to worry seriously about a flow of refugees out of the Soviet Union.

There are no physical barriers to an exodus of the sort that existed until recently between the two Germanies. Moreover, there may be little incentive for the Soviets, given their current economic difficulties, to prevent people from moving westward.

Concentration in Bonn on economic efforts to develop the east German states has not prevented attention there to the poverty and the potential for political instability in Poland, Czechoslovakia and Hungary. Concern about the economies of COMECON nations is nothing new in Bonn. An essential element in *Ostpolitik* was to consider carefully the use of German business ties to keep communication open with productive elements in those countries. Germans have invested heavily in Czechoslovakia and Hungary and are increasingly interested in business possibilities in Poland. Germans have not forgotten that Erich Honecker fell largely as a result of decisions by the Czech and Hungarian governments to allow Germans to flee that repressive regime.

Still, sources of instability in eastern Europe extend far beyond economics. The resurgence of nationalist concerns could do much to disrupt an orderly transformation from communist command systems to democratic demand systems.

In the foreseeable future, the ability of the Germans to influence the course of ethnic tensions will be limited. However, by actively applying lessons learned in east Germany with regard to system transformation, the Germans may well be helpful in making their neighbors' economic readjustments less painful. That, in turn, could help to reduce the intensity of ethnic, religious and other hostilities that have re-emerged in the wake of communist departures. Bilateral activity designed to reduce internecine conflicts in eastern Europe is under way, and is certainly in the best security interest of Germany.

Security for Germany, however, will not be based simply on reacting to events in eastern Europe that remain essentially outside German control. The Germans have set objectives for themselves that consider opportunities to improve stability by taking steps to reduce tensions. These include bilateral diplo-

matic efforts and information programs that stress the capacity
of new political systems to deal with economic problems.

THE GERMAN MILITARY

Germany's military capabilities are substantial and clearly
woven into the government structure in a way that ensures
civilian control. During peacetime, the armed forces are com-
manded by the civilian Minister of Defense. In a military emergency, command of the armed forces would pass to another civilian, the Chancellor. In that situation, the Chancellor would be
aided by a committee of 22 parliamentarians from the German
lower house and 11 from the upper house. That so-called Joint
Committee is one more device to assure military subordination
to civilian authority.

Germany employs a draft, with the term of service recently
having been reduced from 15 to 12 months. Roughly one-half of
the German army is composed of conscripts, while one-third of
the air force and about one-fifth of the navy are draftees. (Table
4.3 shows German forces levels.) German forces have an
impressive record of readiness and efficiency. They are extremely well armed, well trained and highly motivated.

In addition to the active forces, Germany maintains a complicated and efficient reserve system. Equipment and stores
that make this force effective are maintained with care. Regular
training and exercises involving reservists are important elements in German military preparedness.

But German forces by themselves are only a portion of the
important military capabilities that contribute to security of the

TABLE 4.3
German Armed Forces, 1990

Total Active Strength	467,000
Army	308,000
Air Force	106,000
Navy	32,000
Border Guards	20,000
Coast Guard	1,000
Reserves	853,000

Sources: IISS (London) and German Ministry
of Defense.

nation. Integration of German forces into NATO is regarded by almost all interested parties as politically desirable and certainly serves to reinforce Germany's ability to deter military adventure. By treaty, the German armed forces are subordinated to NATO command, even in peacetime (see Appendix 5, the North Atlantic Treaty). Nearly 400,000 non-German troops are stationed in western Germany (see Table 4.1, p. 84).

Admittedly, the future of these forces is far from clear. Eroding threat perceptions and concerns about costs are the logical consequences of Soviet retreat. Orderly rearrangement of western defenses, especially in Germany, is a policy challenge of the first order.

FUTURE SECURITY RELATIONS IN EUROPE

Existing international bodies are likely to provide the framework for future defense arrangements in Europe. The principal organizations concerned are NATO, the Western European Union, the European Community, and, perhaps most important, the Conference on Security and Cooperation in Europe. (See Table 4.4 for membership of these organizations.)

North Atlantic Treaty Organization

The 16-member North Atlantic Treaty Organization, founded in 1947, has been challenged sporadically throughout its existence for a variety of reasons and from a variety of quarters. The most serious crisis occurred in 1966 when the French withdrew their forces from the military structure of the alliance.

Despite these challenges, NATO has been a major stabilizing factor in western Europe. As the military threat from the east recedes, however, political and economic pressures to draw down forces, to slow the purchase of new defense systems or even to dismantle the alliance entirely have come to the forefront in several capitals.

A key consideration in these deliberations about the future of NATO is Germany. The Federal Republic has been the principal European contributor of troops. The strength of the German armed forces has been a major factor in every aspect of NATO politics as well as in NATO strategy and military operations. As previously mentioned, Chancellor Kohl has already announced that the Germans will reduce the troop strength of united

TABLE 4.4
Membership of NATO, WEU, EC, and CSCE

NATO	WEU	EC	CSCE	
Belgium	Belgium	Belgium	Andorra	Netherlands
Canada	France	Denmark	Austria	Norway
Denmark	Germany	France	Belgium	Poland
France	Italy	Germany	Bulgaria	Portugal
Germany	Luxembourg	Greece	Canada	Romania
Greece	Netherlands	Ireland	Cyprus	San Marino
Iceland	Portugal	Italy	Czechoslovakia	Spain
Italy	Spain	Luxembourg	Denmark	Sweden
Luxembourg	UK	Netherlands	Finland	Switzerland
Netherlands		Portugal	France	Turkey
Norway		Spain	Germany	UK
Portugal		UK	Greece	US
Spain			Hungary	USSR
Turkey			Iceland	Yugoslavia
United			Ireland	
Kingdom			Italy	
United			Liechtenstein	
States			Luxembourg	
			Malta	
			Monaco	

Germany to 370,000 and decrease service requirements for conscripts.

In addition, the Federal Republic has been the potential launch site for a number of ground-based nuclear weapons, both missiles and artillery. The decision to abandon the LANCE missile system in the wake of recent developments and the likely role of nuclear artillery as merely a bargaining chip in arms control negotiations create a delicate problem in setting future defense roles. The British and French are attempting, first, to avoid arms control negotiations concerning their own nuclear systems and, second, to operate so as to make nuclearization of the German armed forces unlikely. The Germans themselves clearly have the technical and financial resources to build and deploy nuclear arms. Neither the United States nor any of Germany's neighbors would welcome that prospect. German politicians in the Federal Republic continue to disavow any intention to move in that direction and to stress strong public opposition to such a move. In fact, Foreign Minister Genscher felt compelled to make the following very strong statement just after the Soviets agreed that united Germany could remain in NATO:

Declaration by the Governments of the Federal Republic of Germany and the German Democratic Republic at the Fourth Nuclear Non-Proliferation Treaty Review Conference on 22 August 1990

The Governments of the Federal Republic of Germany and of the German Democratic Republic reaffirm their contractual and unilateral undertaking not to manufacture, possess or have control over nuclear, biological and chemical weapons. They declare that the united Germany too will abide by this obligation.

Rights and obligations under the instruments of the Treaty of 1 July 1968 on the Non-Proliferation of Nuclear Weapons will continue to apply to the united Germany. The united Germany will seek the continued validity of the Non-Proliferation Treaty beyond 1995 and supports the strengthening of the non-proliferation region.

At the Geneva Conference on Disarmament the united Germany will strive for a comprehensive, worldwide and verifiable ban on chemical weapons at the earliest possible date and intends to be one of the original signatories of the Convention.

A review of NATO strategy began before the Berlin Wall fell. At the NATO ministerial meeting in summer 1989, a formal commitment was made to re-examine NATO's flexible response strategy set forth in NATO Military Committee Document MC14/3.

At the June 1990 summit in London, NATO leaders agreed that a formal revision of doctrine was essential. Moreover, they agreed that a rapid move toward elimination of short-range nuclear weapons, especially those that are ground based, was desirable. These weapons have been a major concern for Germans who, during the postwar period of nuclear confrontation, were clearly the primary target for short-range systems located in the communist nation to the east.

Other recent decisions within NATO have special significance for Germany. Drawdowns in the number of foreign troops on German soil and a reduction in the pace of exercises in the wake of the Soviet/Warsaw Pact reductions in force are welcome developments among west Germans who have become increasingly vocal in opposition to low-flying aircraft, jammed road-ways and similar annoyances. Reductions in foreign troops are generally welcome in Germany's larger cities, especially because military garrisons have tied up valuable real estate. On the other hand, many smaller towns that house troops will miss the financial rewards of playing host to allied forces.

Overall, German policy has been clearly directed toward preserving the North Atlantic Treaty Organization and especial-ly toward ensuring that there is no precipitate unilateral with-drawal of U.S. troops from central Europe. German armed forces remain within the NATO command structure, and German defense spending continues to be substantial. Estimates of 1990 spending run to more than $30 billion, although reductions as great as 4 percent are forecast in 1991.

Germans have performed well in a variety of policymaking positions in NATO. The present Secretary General of the entire alliance and a principal troop commander who controls all allied forces in central Europe are two notable examples of German leadership.

> "I believe that the Americans will insist—and correctly insist—on a more coherent European pillar to the alliance. I believe that our own self-respect as Europeans also requires this."
>
> Senior British official to a German audience, fall 1990

The German armed forces will remain in num-ber second only to France in western Europe. Al-though some further re-ductions in German troop strength may occur, it is likely that any such reductions will be undertaken after close consultation with Germany's various allies.

Concerns in Bonn about deploying non-German troops east of the Elbe are shared in Brussels and other NATO capitals. At present, western military and police forces in the territory that was formerly under communist domination are all German. Withdrawal of Soviet troops is continuing, albeit slowly. No immediate plans exist to extend non-German NATO forces into the states of eastern Germany.

Germany's frontiers with Poland, Czechoslovakia and Austria remain essentially undefended. This may change if large-scale westward migration into Germany occurs as a result of economic problems or political instability in eastern Europe.

Germany enjoys support for its continued participation in NATO from a variety of other European states. Indeed, once the Soviet Union ended its opposition to NATO membership for unified Germany, Warsaw Pact allies, including Poland, Czechoslovakia and Hungary, openly expressed such support. There is little talk now of "keeping the Germans down," and there is definitely sentiment, in Paris and elsewhere, that removing Germany from the NATO command structure would be highly undesirable politically as well as militarily.

The clear change in the European military situation makes re-evaluation of NATO strategy and force posture not only desirable but also politically inevitable. However, to assume that NATO will wither is to ignore the fact that the Soviet Union will continue to be by far the most powerful military force in Europe. From a German perspective, NATO, with the United States as its primary counterweight to Soviet nuclear capabilities, will continue to be a critical organization. Modifications within the alliance toward multinational forces, toward lower levels of forces and toward highly mobile forces will proceed. The alliance's fundamental political functions are unlikely to be eroded quickly.

> *"Our neighbors accept German military strength only because German forces are firmly implanted in the NATO security structure."*
>
> Senior German
> Security Specialist

Beyond internal modifications, NATO is likely to continue to play a key role in arms control negotiations; to provide a forum for discussion as a new security order emerges in Europe; to offer reassurance to Germany's neighbors; and, especially as the WEU and the EC become more important in the security dimension, to provide a way to keep the United States involved in Europe. Even the Soviet Union has expressed appreciation, albeit grudging, that NATO is a stabilizing influence in Europe.

One problem that has persisted in NATO and that is especially acute for Germany is the so-called out of area question. The North Atlantic Treaty, as amended, specifically limits activities of the alliance to Europe, the North Atlantic and its littoral, the Mediterranean, and Turkey.

Many see the German Basic Law as constricting the Chancellor's capacity to dispatch German troops except under

NATO auspices. The Chancellor has committed himself to a constitutional amendment that would recognize the sovereignty enjoyed by the new, unified Germany, now out from under four-power constraints (see Appendix 6, "Treaty on the Final Settlement with Respect to Germany").

Amending the German Constitution requires a two-thirds absolute majority in both houses of Parliament. At present, the ruling coalition does not possess the numbers required to make such a change. The opposition SPD has stipulated that it would not support a constitutional change regarding the armed forces unless troops are restricted to operations under UN auspices. The socialists are inclined to tie constitutional modifications concerning the armed forces to constitutional guarantees on other issues ranging from abortion to social welfare.

German security concerns obviously extend beyond Europe. Germany's dependence on raw materials from abroad and a German economy that derives one-third of its income from exports combine to make situations like the Persian Gulf war especially important to German leaders and to the German public. But the constitutional and treaty restrictions emerging from World War II continue to limit employment of German forces.

That situation has provided new impetus to the Western European Union. A brief look at its emerging role is instructive in terms of future security arrangements.

Western European Union

Germany is one of nine NATO and EC members that compose the Western European Union. The organization was founded in 1948 and enlarged to include Germany and Italy in 1954. Its provisions for automatic military assistance in the event of an armed attack against any one of its members do not specify that any defensive activity be confined to the European continent.

In practice, the WEU surrendered most of its operational functions to NATO in the early 1950s. But in 1987, during the Iranian attempt to disrupt oil supplies by mining the Persian Gulf, the Western European Union became the focal point for coordination of non-U.S. allied activity designed to keep sea lanes open. In the process, the organization took on new life. Regular meetings are now conducted among military chiefs of staff and their subordinates. Logistics for operations in the

Persian Gulf are increasingly multinational. The Western European Union has played a key coordinating role in those arrangements. Although ministers have been meeting regularly since 1984, the WEU's ability to act in support of U.S. naval operations in the Persian Gulf in the late 1980s raised the organization's profile and revitalized it.

The Western European Union differs from NATO in two significant ways. The first and most obvious is that the United States is not a member. Second, as previously mentioned, is the lack of any geographic restrictions on WEU activities.

Germany has participated fully and enthusiastically in the policy deliberations of the WEU. In addition, within the limits of its constitutional constraints, Germany has supported the WEU's two principal military activities. The first, in 1987, was designed to protect shipping from the consequences of the Iran-Iraq war and involved German agreement to send naval vessels into the Mediterranean to relieve other nations' ships that were proceeding into the Gulf for minesweeping and escort duties. The second, during the crisis following Iraq's invasion of Kuwait, involved German efforts to support opposition to Saddam Hussein and to reverse his seizure of Kuwait. As a WEU member, but based on a unilateral decision, Germany sent minesweeping ships into the eastern Mediterranean in late 1990 to free other NATO members to operate forces in the Persian Gulf. In addition, Germany's decision to provide major financial support for U.S. operations in the Gulf, the contribution of air and sea transport capabilities, logistic support and communications and engineering equipment, and the donation of specialized reconnaissance vehicles to U.S. forces in the Saudi Arabian desert were undertaken after consultation within the framework of the Western European Union.

Given NATO's inability to function in similar situations, and given the likelihood that Saddam Hussein's aggression will not be the last affecting the broad interests of European countries, the WEU will probably continue to play a role in such situations. The French, in particular, are pleased that the European states, acting in concert but not necessarily under international command, have been able to contribute militarily in complex and dangerous situations. Other WEU members, while not overtly criticizing NATO, have made a point of coordinating their policy decisions within WEU fora.

The combination of structural attributes and political circumstances that led to WEU's reinvigoration may swell sentiment in favor of a purely European defense organization that could create a challenge to NATO as the predominant security organization in Europe. Given the U.S. absence, evolution of the Western European Union would do little to improve U.S.-German cooperation on defense questions in times of scarce resources. That is a key consideration not just for the United States and Germany but also for Germany's neighbors.

European Community

At the same time that the WEU is branching out, the European Community is expanding its range of interests. France and Germany have expanded consultations on both foreign and defense policies, raising the possibility that the European Community may become more vigorous regarding questions of security. French-German cooperation on defense is not a new development. Although efforts by the Germans and the British to encourage the French to rejoin the military structure of the NATO alliance have not succeeded, joint German-French activities including the formation of a Franco-German brigade reflect the desire of leaders in both nations to address security questions on a European basis.

The revitalization of the Western European Union and the nascent process of expanding the scope and responsibilities of the European Community highlight shifting power realities within the North Atlantic alliance. Europeans, feeling less threatened and better off, wish to set their own terms for the role that the United States will play as leader or as at least an equal in continental defense structures. Given post-World War II history and current nuclear realities, equality is a problematic concept. There is no denying, however, the move toward coordination, if not consolidation, of European positions on defense.

President Mitterrand and Chancellor Kohl issued a joint letter in December 1990 setting forth the desirability of careful coordination of foreign and defense policies among members of the European Community. In that connection, they recommended close consultation between the Western European Union and the European Community. The two leaders also recommended that the role of the European Parliament be strengthened to take into account security issues ranging from immigration to organized crime.

The Italian Foreign Minister proposed that there be a formal merger of the European Community and the Western European Union. That would require a modification of the Treaty of Rome of 1957, which established the European Community as a body primarily concerned with nondefense matters. The Italian proposal did not generate widespread support.

One complication in attempting to merge the two bodies is that three members of the European Community, Greece, Denmark and neutral Ireland, are not members of the Western European Union. In addition, many of the most attractive potential EC members are neutral. Abstention on defense questions is one suggested way to protect neutrality. Even though WEU membership could easily be extended to the three countries just noted, overlapping functions could well cause friction between the two organizations, especially among bureaucrats protecting turf.

Discussion within the European Community about a move to encompass security concerns stressed four principal items. First, arms control would be taken under EC purview. Then, research and development on military materiel, military export policies, and the creation and operation of joint peacekeeping forces that could operate outside NATO would be brought under EC oversight.

Not all Europeans support these proposals. It is clear that one of the consequences of a substantial increase in EC activity on defense issues would be to cause the United States, not a member of the European Community, some anxiety. At a time when the perception of threat to western Europe is declining in the United States at least as quickly as it is on the continent, actions that would undermine NATO would not be welcomed by most in the U.S. Congress. Indeed, the pressures for U.S. military spending as a result of the 1990-91 crisis in the Persian Gulf, combined with a stubborn budget deficit, will cause many in Congress to question whether the United States should continue large military expenditures designed primarily to reinforce European security.

Germany in its new unified status, facing security dilemmas to the east and uncertainties about security-related spending to the west, is in a difficult position. Germany is increasingly the leader of the European Community. A move toward a greater defense role for that organization can only weaken NATO. Weakening NATO not only could reinvigorate Soviet concern about German military strength, but also could seriously threaten U.S. support for the alliance.

Reaction within Germany to the proposals to strengthen the EC's security activities has been mixed. Generally, informed observers have stressed that while declarations of intent are one kind of activity, implementing policies is quite another.

Reaction in Washington to shifts in the WEU and the EC has generally been muted. The alliance is a familiar symbol that continues to generate substantial support in Washington. Budget debates in Washington, however, will undoubtedly focus renewed attention on what could be interpreted as a European move away from NATO.

Germany has no choice but to play a major role in whatever arrangements emerge. Because of its economic and military strength, its geographic position and the necessity that it resume its historical role as a bridge to the east, Germany can lower its defense profile, but only at substantial political and, to some degree, military risk.

An overall security architecture for Europe, however, cannot be built simply on the basis of developments in the west. The desirability, if not the necessity, of including the Soviet Union in any eventual "European settlement" is undeniable. With that in mind, a fourth organization is growing in importance in the eyes of those concerned with preserving peace and prosperity in Europe. That organization is the Conference on Security and Cooperation in Europe.

Conference on Security and Cooperation in Europe

Security in its broadest sense is based upon political and economic relationships that offer confidence and predictability in an uncertain world. A Europe divided between an affluent and self-confident west and an impoverished, chaotic east is not a secure environment for parties on either side.

Given the state of flux in Europe, any talk of European "architecture" is probably not instructive in the near term. The notion of a security "regime," however, is a useful concept.

The Conference on Security and Cooperation in Europe is an important effort toward building a security regime. This broad organization, which includes both the United States and the

Soviet Union, has virtues and vices. But it is receiving increased attention as a possible umbrella not only for military forces but also for the overall concerns of policymakers seeking stability and security.

For 15 years, when difficult problems have arisen in Europe, a tendency has existed to bring together divergent viewpoints emanating, on the one hand, from Moscow and its allies and, on the other, from western Europe and the United States. That effort has resulted in a series of meetings under the aegis of the loosely constructed CSCE.

Given the frequently contrasting views of the members and the lack of a formal charter, the absence of a formal bureaucratic structure for CSCE is neither surprising nor necessarily, at least until this point, undesirable. The focus of CSCE activity has been threefold: military relationships, economic relationships and human rights questions. The organization's wide-reaching membership and its ability to compare behavior of member states against ideals proclaimed in conference have been a welcome organizing device in dialogue about security-related matters in Europe.

Progress in reducing tensions along these three dimensions has been spotty. Still, participating nations have brought controversial concerns to the CSCE forum with the clear understanding that there would be no binding resolutions at the conclusion of deliberations that might cause CSCE members pain and suffering after the fact.

Fundamental differences between communist-dominated states and those in the west, while clearly not ignored, have not been insurmountable obstacles to meaningful discourse. Although a high level of generality is necessary to accommodate contrasting positions, and although policy decisions on controversial issues are rare, the CSCE process is, in conception and performance, a "confidence-building measure."

Perhaps the most important characteristic of CSCE is its members' clear acceptance of the idea that military questions, economic issues and concerns about human rights are inexorably connected. Open discussion of these topics has reduced the potential for misunderstanding and conflict between east and west.

The remarkable success of negotiations on conventional forces in Europe (CFE) is the most dramatic example to date of CSCE activity. Twenty-two of the 34 members agreed under

CSCE auspices to a treaty that specifies significant reductions in many types of military equipment, thereby sharply limiting the potential for military action on the continent (see Table 4.5). Further, members agreed informally that talks on the elimination of short-range nuclear weapons and on troop ceilings would follow.

The conventional force reduction talks have been greeted with enthusiasm throughout Germany. The announcement of agreement in principle, appearing as it did on October 3, 1990, the day of German unification, was a strong signal that Europe is becoming a safer place. Subsequent endorsement of the agreement at the ministerial level strengthened the optimism built during 19 months of successful negotiations. Formal treaty ratification and implementation remain to be accomplished and will be problematical at best. The pace of Soviet withdrawal from east Germany may be a particularly sensitive issue.

Perhaps the greatest problem in regarding CSCE as a primary vehicle for improving security across Europe is the continuing requirement for unanimity for most of its decisions. No organization composed of 34 or more members, each of which has veto power, is likely to be able to produce binding policy declarations, implement policy or reach consensus about what constitutes progress.

Experience in the EC Council of Ministers, however, has provided support for optimists who argue that a wide range of issues that might become CSCE concerns could be decided on a

TABLE 4.5
CFE Treaty Agreement

	November 1990			1994		
	Warsaw Pact	Soviet Union	NATO	Warsaw Pact	Soviet Union	NATO
Tanks	39,000	21,000	26,650	20,000	13,150	20,000
Combat vehicles	48,000	32,000	34,500	30,000	20,000	30,000
Artillery	32,000	18,000	21,200	20,000	13,200	20,000
Combat aircraft	8,500	6,700	6,100	6,800	5,150	6,800

Note: The 22 signatories are NATO's 16 members and 6 from the Warsaw Pact.
Source: Treaty text.

majority basis. But majority rule in CSCE is unlikely to emerge in the near future.

More immediate questions include whether, in order to make CSCE more effective, there must be an erosion of NATO's predominant position on defense questions. There is little enthusiasm for such a prospect in most NATO capitals, and marked concern about such a possibility in some, especially Washington and London.

In Bonn, however, CSCE is seen as a possible means of deliverance from the problem that Germans have faced historically and face anew. German security depends on good relations between that country and neighbors both east and west. CSCE is the only organization that presently offers access to all the parties most likely to contest German interests in Europe. It is not surprising, therefore, that in November the German Chancellor and his Foreign Minister enthusiastically endorsed not only the successful result of negotiations in Vienna over conventional forces in Europe, but also the concept that CSCE could become a guarantor of democracy as "the only form of government" in Europe as well as a vehicle for movement toward free market economies throughout the continent. German support for establishment of a secretariat for CSCE, of annual meetings of foreign ministers and biannual summits, and of a center for conflict resolution in Vienna, or perhaps subsequently in Helsinki, is noteworthy.

Following declarations that proceeded from the November meeting in Paris, German Foreign Minister Genscher made a point of stressing the important role the United States would play in any developments under CSCE. He emphasized the history of cooperation among allies on both sides of the Atlantic based on close political, historical and cultural, as well as economic, ties. He added further language about the undesirability of protectionism and about the need to safeguard peace. However, he made no specific reference to relations among NATO, the Western European Union, the European Community, and new entities conceived as elements of CSCE.

Ideally, of course, CSCE could evolve as a complementary security system in which NATO could eventually be enveloped. The communication, consultation and cooperation that have characterized CSCE activities to date provide a model for future moves to reduce misunderstandings. But practical questions arise when roles that CSCE might successfully play are considered.

For example, how will CSCE relate to the post-1992 European Community? Can NATO function under a board of directors composed of at least 34 members, many of whom do not share its fundamental history, values or future outlook? Can CSCE take into account the out of area questions that are so troubling today? Moreover, basic questions about whether CSCE members will submit to arbitration of disputes remain unanswered.

It is important for European states, including Germany, to encourage solicitous behavior on the part of both the United States and the Soviet Union in situations such as the Persian Gulf war. Europe is fundamentally resource dependent, and the United States and the Soviet Union will always have a say about whether the economic prosperity that has emerged in Europe is to continue apace. Even the most cynical analyst, however, must acknowledge that it is in the interest of both the United States and the Soviet Union to see to it that Europe continues to prosper.

Philosophical and organizational difficulties aside, CSCE is a starting point for a European security regime that can include both the Soviet Union and the United States in a way that seemed a dim hope, if not a delusion, only a few months ago. Policymakers in the United States are not blind to the necessity to adjust to Germany's new strengths.

These new realities must be a cornerstone of relations between the United States and Germany. If U.S.-German relations are to prosper, Germans must be in a position to accept responsibility commensurate with their economic might and political influence.

Certainly, Soviet internal distress could spill over into eastern Europe and from there into neutral states and even Germany itself. But manipulation of European politics to serve Soviet goals appears at present to be outside the realm of Moscow's capabilities.

The same is generally true about the United States. U.S. policy preferences will continue to be very important in European circles. The continued existence of a U.S. nuclear capability, unpleasant to contemplate but necessary to understand, remains the ultimate guarantor against Soviet truancy in the military realm. By including both superpowers in the CSCE regime, European states, especially Germany, have some access to the thinking that must precede behavior on the part of either of the two military giants.

OUTLOOK

Optimists observing the European scene take comfort from the erosion of ideological tension between east and west and from the scrambled but dynamic development of institutions in the west concerned with security. Competition among multinational institutions for influence on security questions is likely to continue, if not to intensify.

Official German positions stress the continuing importance of NATO, albeit a NATO with an unspecified new strategy. Even Gorbachev has expressed his enthusiasm for the alliance and for continued American participation in it. It is clear that American capacity to sway, if not to constrain, Germany is something that the Soviets regard as welcome.

Germany's relative influence in the alliance, however, is bound to increase. U.S. preoccupation with situations elsewhere in the world, sentiment within Congress to reduce defense spending in general and spending on Europe in particular, and U.S. troop drawdowns in connection with arms control agreements combine to reduce U.S. ability to drive alliance decisions.

French-German cooperation on defense questions, both on a bilateral basis and within the European Community, is a significant development directly related to the future of NATO. Because France remains outside the military structure of the alliance, French-German cooperation on multinational troop formations is one more indication of German intentions to steer a more independent course on security matters. Even if a strong defense component of EC activity does not emerge, and even if common foreign policies among Community members remain elusive, French-German cooperation continues to be a significant element in EC contributions to security.

German attitudes toward the Western European Union have been ambivalent. Heavy stress appears in most policy pronouncements on the importance of including the United States in any security activity in which Germany might engage. The U.S. absence from the WEU has caused the Germans to turn toward NATO when difficult policy questions have arisen. German preference for NATO as a security forum is understandable in view of both treaty arrangements and the German Constitution, and it is likely to continue.

On the other hand, Kohl was the first western statesman to endorse CSCE as a vehicle for security cooperation. In his 10-point plan of November 1989, he recommended that there be an institutionalization of CSCE processes and the creation of a Center for Conflict Prevention operated by that organization. One of the principal attractions of CSCE for the Germans is that both the United States and the Soviet Union can be included in discussions. The success of talks on conventional force strength involving the United States, the Soviet Union and their respective allies in NATO and the Warsaw Pact is greeted in Germany as an indicator of the Chancellor's foresightedness. CSCE has the added advantage of being able to encompass ecological questions, genetic engineering, information programs, surveillance of human rights compliance, and a variety of other nonmilitary topics that affect security, even if only indirectly.

Adjustments in institutional prerogatives and membership will take time and will likely give new meaning to the term "bureaucratic turf." Political, economic, cultural, and military factors will make policy hard to execute and progress hard to measure. One key characteristic of all institutional change in the European environment will be an increased role for Germany as leader.

Institutional dynamics are, however, unlikely to distract Germans from more fundamental realities. Present German leaders do not assume that the Soviets will be inclined to pursue political and economic reform with vigor and consistency. Even if they are so inclined, Soviet leaders may well find themselves constrained in unfamiliar ways by popular opinion.

Germans recognize clearly that if the Soviet transformation into a more liberal, demand-based system is to succeed, the Germans must be primary economic partners. Treaties between Bonn and Moscow proliferated in late 1990. A friendship treaty, a transition treaty on financial matters and a treaty on cooperation in business, industry, science, and technology all evidence concern for stability in the Soviet Union among the Germans. Those treaty arrangements do not, however, eliminate formidable Soviet nuclear and conventional military capabilities, nor has there been evidence that those treaties have accelerated the pace of withdrawal of Soviet troops from east Germany.

Germany's near neighbors to the east face difficulties similar to those affecting Moscow. In Poland, Czechoslovakia and Hungary, moves toward democratization and economic reorganization do not obscure nationalist conflicts, governments' inability to live up to popular expectations for economic development, or social and ethnic tensions. Unrest in those countries could very quickly spread to eastern Germany or reinforce dissatisfaction there, both major security considerations for Bonn/Berlin.

Tension, conflict and even hostilities in Romania, Bulgaria and Yugoslavia are not minor factors in Germans' calculus about their own security. Germans see unrest in those places as threatening in two primary ways. First, massive immigration to the west could become a problem. Second, Germans are sensitive to Soviet anxieties about unrest in the Balkans and worry about Soviet military actions there.

In summary, German concerns about developments in the east make abundantly clear the need to maintain strong ties with Germany's allies in the west, including the United States. Policy choices leading in that direction are, however, more easily stated than pursued.

Germany's political emergence, based on its economic strength and diplomatic foresight, has created expectations among its allies about a variety of security questions. German domestic divisions over the Persian Gulf war, reflected in demonstrations and policy debates, have led to resentment in Washington and dissatisfaction in both Paris and London, although German financial support was welcomed.

The bittersweet character of unified Germany's emergence as a great power is evident in a situation like that in the Persian Gulf where U.S. interest in world order is primary while European order dominates German thinking. The ramifications of the German Basic Law's prohibition on military activity beyond self-defense may well reverberate for a prolonged period in the institutions previously described. Perceived German reluctance to support the Gulf coalition generated popular antipathy toward the new Germany in the United States and elsewhere.

It will take intense consultation and careful collaboration if U.S. and German policymakers are to maintain the friendly atmosphere that has characterized most relations between the two countries during the past four decades. The security dimension of U.S.-German relations, connected intimately as it is with the economic dimension, will develop in a positive way only if there are successful moves toward understanding on both sides of the Atlantic.

These efforts cannot succeed in the medium and long terms if they are limited to government activity. Diplomacy and defense coordination are key, but private sector support for government programs, cooperation on defense procurement and production, and equitable sharing of the costs of defense are also necessary.

Popular support for continued cordial relations between Germany and the United States depends on shared perceptions of progress in each of these areas. Those perceptions, in turn, proceed from effective private and public communications on priorities, policies and cultural sensitivities.

CHAPTER FIVE

United Germany and the United States

Myriad changes have occurred recently within Germany and within the economic and security environments in which united Germany must develop. Focus on change could, however, obscure underlying continuities that are fundamental to the future of U.S.-German relations.

Postwar cooperation between the two countries has been based on dedication to the preservation of each country's democratic political order. Further, the postwar traditions of military alliance and of economic and political cooperation between America and Germany have been quite strong. The military aspect of that cooperation within the NATO framework has often captured center stage, at times eclipsing economic considerations. Yet the establishment and growth of healthy west European economies was a necessary precondition for military cooperation.

The Marshall Plan for European economic reconstruction was based directly on preconceived political goals. The establishment of the federal German political system was undertaken with a keen eye toward sustaining economic redevelopment while preventing emergence of another authoritarian regime in Germany. The unprecedented U.S. generosity during those times was not without self-interest. The capacity to sustain democratically oriented German leaders during a period of privation and centrifugal political tendencies within Germany reflected Washington policymakers' clear realization that an economically strong Germany was the key to maintaining stability and security in Europe as a whole. Soviet postwar behavior reinforced that notion and led to both the reintroduction of large numbers of U.S. forces on the continent and to the development of the North Atlantic Treaty Organization.

Inclusion of Germany in that military structure in 1955 involved a series of difficult political decisions not only by American leaders but also by policymakers in Britain, France and other neighbors of Germany west of the so-called Iron Curtain. The Cold War rhetoric, with its emphasis on military threat, proceeded in no small measure from the necessity to generate the political will and economic wherewithal from populations on both sides of the Atlantic to provide a non-nuclear defense of western Europe. Sustained economic growth was a precondition for the way in which NATO doctrine evolved, and especially for the capacity to develop conventional forces compatible with the NATO flexible response strategy. Germany became a territorial and political cornerstone of that strategy.

Clearly, Germany will remain a fulcrum for construction of a stable security environment in Europe as a whole. Its economic strength and central position necessitate an activist German role in rebuilding eastern Europe. The most likely near-term danger to even greater prosperity among the western European states would be a renewed security threat from the Soviet Union. Implosion there could renew Soviet military pressure on eastern Europe. Simultaneously, the *relative* influence of the United States in European economic, political and military affairs has declined and is likely to continue to do so.

Those policymakers contemplating changes in international organizations that affect Germany, its European neighbors and its North American allies do seek to take into account these developments. But structural endpoints or anything resembling final organizational solutions in the economic and security environments in Europe are not now in view. Because of the uncertainty about appropriate policies to achieve stability and security in Europe, bilateral cooperation between Germany and the United States is essential. Neither the state of flux within Germany, nor the regional and global power shifts, nor the changing U.S. propensities and policies should be allowed to obscure that fundamental relationship.

COMMON VALUES

It is thought-provoking to reflect on the language of the U.S. founding fathers when examining how Germany reacts to its changing European environment. Within Germany itself, within the European Community and within the broad range of organizations designed to provide stability and security on the European continent, the notions of life, liberty and the pursuit of happiness are alive and well. Priorities of nation-states and international organizations alike include forming more perfect unions, establishing justice and ensuring domestic tranquility, providing for common defense, and promoting the general welfare.

Further, these goals reflect emphasis on process rather than on any eventual state of perfection. Priorities differ among nations and among international organizations. There is often distance among goals, policies and resources. No current German leader, however, could survive politically by contesting the authenticity of such human aspirations as were set forth in America in the 18th century.

There are those who will argue that the period between World War II and the present is insufficiently long to provide a basis upon which confidently to reject German tendencies toward authoritarianism. Nonetheless, a combination of German democratic performance since World War II, the utter failure of the communist experiment, the economic interdependence among advanced industrialized nations, and the increasing translucency of governmental activities as a result of television and other media makes it not only improbable but also impractical for Germans to turn away sharply from democratic values.

Differences in history and culture notwithstanding, those values form the basis for both the U.S. and the German polities and will make it likely that disagreements that do evolve between the two states will concern priorities, policies and implementation rather than fundamentals. Intense hostility or resentment will, it is hoped, be rare. When disputes arise, many will stem from lack of cultural understanding or from poor information. Discord of greatest concern will emerge when there is competition for economic advantage and/or political influence.

Despite differences between a parliamentary system like Germany's and the U.S. federal system, continued firsthand communication between members of legislatures can be an extremely productive activity. Bilateral exchanges of members and staff between Germany and the United States continue. Similar exchanges of parliamentarians that extend beyond the Bundestag, the Bundesrat, the U.S. House, and the U.S. Senate are equally important. For example, parliamentarians from the North Atlantic Assembly and the EC Parliament have exchanged visits and views. The expenses involved in these exchanges are well justified in a time of political and economic flux. German and U.S. political figures can continue to be both influential and effective in these fora. Their connections enrich the bilateral dialogue between Germany and the United States. Activity in the United Nations and in the various multilateral political, economic and security organizations also fosters creative approaches to new problems.

Issues that might arise at the governmental level often receive more public attention than the critically important day-to-day business activities that connect Germany and the United States. Multinational corporations, long significant adjuncts to governmental communication, are increasingly important throughout the industrialized world. U.S.-German cooperation in multinational business activities has been a model for the growing interdependence that characterizes the international economy.

Major German and American financial institutions are sources of ideas and initiatives that have allowed governmental policy preferences to be realized. Chemical, pharmaceutical, telecommunications, and similar companies on both sides of the Atlantic provide connections for manufacturing and services industries. These connections improve the overall quality of U.S.-German relations in immeasurable ways.

The human element in corporate activity is an important factor in productive communication among industrialized countries. The increasing mobility of highly educated and highly skilled people of varying nationalities, especially in the more technical industries, improves cultural understanding and facilitates exchanges of cutting edge technologies. Peripatetic executives provide both an underpinning and an incentive for forward-looking exchanges of ideas in both the public and the private sectors. German-American cooperation in this respect has been long-standing and productive. Among those industries with lengthy histories of cooperation are accounting, banking, telecommunications, consulting, finance, manufacturing, and transportation.

Communication between German and American labor organizations is another time-tested activity that has furthered U.S.-German understanding. Especially given the positive role that unions can play in easing the social adjustments under way in eastern Germany and eastern Europe, such ties continue to be valuable.

Existing nongovernmental connections reinforce basic political and economic commonalities and ameliorate the potential for conflict or misunderstanding. Among the policy areas that benefit from communication are:

- current and developing U.S. overseas investment in western and eastern Europe;

- international linkages of interest rates and exchange rates;

- development of markets in eastern Europe; and

- shared concerns about continued growth in western economies.

OUTLOOK

Four situations could, nevertheless, be especially challenging in the near and medium term.

- First, sensing its geometric increase in economic influence in Europe, Germany may acquiesce in or, worse, lead a European move toward protectionism that would work to the disadvantage of the United States.

- Second, emergence of intensified protectionist sentiment within the United States based on perceived competitive advantage of the Europeans could breed stress if not hostility.

- Third, if Germany fails to participate in global police actions like that in the Persian Gulf, significant U.S. resentment could emerge. That, in turn, could lead to degradation or even abnegation of the U.S. commitment to ensure European security.

- Fourth, German anxiety and frustration with political developments along its periphery, especially to the east, could lead to an increase in German armed strength. The

U.S. stake in preventing German-Soviet confrontation would be great, and differences between the United States and Germany could become manifest.

It is not possible to assign even parametric probabilities to these speculations. A brief reflection on each, however, might be useful to policymakers in Washington and Bonn/Berlin as they endeavor to reinforce U.S.-German consultation and cooperation and minimize misunderstanding.

There is no question that a Europe of 320 million people, unified under a variety of international structures, could develop a trading regime that emphasizes protection of European industries and labor forces at the expense of any outside producers. Community intransigence in the GATT agricultural negotiations, EC domestic content regulations and Community-wide standards have led to concern within the United States that non-EC nations could be hurt by design or by error as the EC's single market process matures. If progress toward 1992 continues at its present pace, the ability to orchestrate tariffs, establish quotas, enforce discriminatory regulations on various products and services, and generally resist free trade could develop further.

Germany, as Europe's leading producer, is heavily dependent on its positive balance of trade. As its neighbors become more and more closely tied to its economic engine, Germany could choose to emulate Japan in a variety of ways, including continued or increased subsidization of industry, research and development, and agriculture. The German inclination to move in that direction may be accentuated by poor economic performance in the United States. Persistent U.S. budget deficits and weakened foreign trade together with the necessity to repair its financial industry and to come to grips with problems in education could cause some Germans to regard the United States less favorably as an economic leader.

Developments along these lines would, of course, create an outcry within the U.S. Congress and eventually build resentment among Americans in general. Resultant animosity could have a very negative effect on U.S.-German cooperation and could lead to a general increase in tension between the two nations.

U.S. frustration resulting from an inability to come to grips with the fundamental problems just described could intensify sentiment in favor of protectionist legislation and practices. There are strong protectionist voices in Congress.

The GATT's uncertain future has attracted little public attention in America. The current capacity of the Administration to draw trade agreements quickly and without interference from congressional amendments provides some slim hope that the benefits of GATT can be preserved. If that authority were to expire, the prospect of reaching an agreement in the Uruguay Round of negotiations would likely also expire. This would lend volume to the populist and protectionist voices in Congress.

Further, the downward trend in U.S. defense spending can be expected to resume when military activity in the Gulf ends. Americans increasingly perceive Europeans, and especially Germans, as more than capable of providing for their own defenses. Similarly, the CFE agreement makes congressional leaders hesitant to push for improved defense capabilities in Europe. That hesitancy persists in spite of slow Soviet execution of troop withdrawals agreed to in the November 1990 Paris meeting of the CSCE.

Efforts in the United States to maintain domestic standards of living and modernize an aging industrial base are real. To help realize these goals, lawmakers might seek to augment revenues or to preserve jobs in some sectors by imposing substantial duties on foreign goods. The result would be a general deterioration in overall economic relations that could not fail to affect U.S.-German cooperation.

The growing economic leverage of Germany in the wake of unification, accentuated by the decline of the Soviet Union and the strengthening of the European Community, is also likely to generate opinion in the United States that Germany should shoulder a greater portion of the burden of ensuring international peace. However, the provisions of the Basic Law do not clearly permit the employment of German forces outside Germany. The acts of unification have not clarified that situation.

Defense specialists in the United States are watching this situation with interest. The Chancellor has committed himself in principle to seeking amendment of the Basic Law, but has set no time frame. Although some pressures for quick movement have developed in the U.S. Congress, especially given the experience of the Persian Gulf war, most leaders in the House and

Senate recognize that Germans today are most anxious to steer their own course in international affairs without undue pressure from abroad.

As problems of unification are resolved, however, and as Germany continues to grow economically stronger and enjoy even greater prosperity, U.S. leaders and the American public will likely want Germany to look after its own interests in contributing to international stability. German participation in multilateral force structures and in contingency operations outside Europe will be considered minimum contributions to international security.

While any willingness of Germany to share the risks and expenses of military operations is likely to be welcome in Washington, the possibility that the effects of instability in eastern Europe could provoke significant increases in German force levels is a matter of some concern. The weakness of the Soviet Union, the apparent limited interest of western investors in eastern Europe and Germany's concentration on modernization of its own eastern states combine to make economic progress in eastern Europe halting at best.

The popular optimism that followed communism's demise in Poland, Czechoslovakia and Hungary is fast eroding, and economic performance in those countries is falling substantially short of expectations. This classic recipe for political unrest has many in Washington as well as in Germany watchful, if not worried.

German concerns, however, are more immediate. The likelihood that economic modernization can take place at a rapid pace in eastern Germany without being affected by developments in Poland, Czechoslovakia and Hungary is slim indeed. Should German policymakers decide that it will be necessary to strengthen border controls, and should Germans become so concerned with political unrest in their own country that they move forces eastward, the potential for deteriorating relations between Germany and the Soviet Union is substantial. Barring an unforeseeable significant reduction in all nuclear systems, the United States would have a strong interest in the effects that deteriorating German-Soviet relations might have on global stability.

Optimists considering the four potential dilemmas outlined above are bound to object to their gloomy character. They will certainly stress the steady growth of the west European economy and the responsible behavior of Germans in the Federal Republic in policy decisions since 1949.

Further, increased tensions do not necessarily mean a net deterioration in relations. Difficulties that might arise in connection with any of the four issue areas certainly would be addressed with enthusiasm and alacrity once recognized. However, the initial stages of each are likely to be quite subtle. For them to be recognized, therefore, considerable attention must be devoted to nurturing America's changing relationship with Germany.

Greater danger lies in some combination of the four situations described. Reciprocal protectionism is certainly not unknown. Irritation over questions of military burden sharing is also a familiar phenomenon. In addition, there is no denying that the fractious atmosphere in eastern Europe has been a major factor historically in German security considerations and will continue to be so. Perhaps the greatest danger is thus the risk that the United States will ignore such developments until it is too late to influence their course.

The challenge in U.S.-German relations, then, lies in maintaining open communication and a willingness to address difficult situations through consultation and, in most cases, likely agreement. The process of unification requires U.S. policymakers to realize that Germany has earned an enhanced role as a world leader.

The emergence of unified Germany as the central power in Europe need not be viewed with alarm. German political and economic power has increased dramatically. The Germans have demonstrated their commitment to democracy and have shown themselves to be responsible and responsive allies. Their greater freedom of action will demand sensitivity and understanding from U.S. leaders. Commensurate German military responsibilities in the world are likely to follow. This requires careful attention to German views on economic and security questions.

Germany will be a major factor in maintaining good relations between the United States and the European Community. Continuation of Germany's current role in facilitating communication between Washington and Brussels will become increasingly important as the century turns.

The United States has not abdicated its leadership role; it has moved closer to achieving its postwar economic, political and security goals. But success has its price. One part of that price is re-evaluating the policies that brought the United States and its European friends this far.

It has been difficult over the past 40 years to lead a consensus against a communist system that confronted and challenged western basic ideals and values. However, not only did America have enormous economic, political and military strength, but also most in the west could see relatively clearly the consequences that could result from losing the struggle against communism.

The situation today is significantly more demanding. U.S. influence on international affairs is no longer as strong as in the immediate post-World War II era, especially in relative economic terms. But shifting patterns of economic influence need not be read as prophecies that the United States is in inexorable decline. The more interesting trend is the increase in productivity and relative influence among U.S. allies and friends. George Marshall and other U.S. leaders of his era may well have foreseen such developments.

The American model of industrial development is being modified constantly as other advanced nations press for competitive advantage. Economic organizations like the European Community, and economic systems that overtly combine government and industrial interests as in Japan, can be expected to develop goals and priorities different from those of the United States.

A major challenge to U.S. policymakers lies in understanding the differences between U.S. priorities and those of its main economic partners and competitors. Europe and Japan can be expected to differ between themselves and with the United States on a number of economic issues ranging from trade to intellectual property rights.

The erosion of Soviet influence will make consensus between Europe and the United States increasingly elusive unless the Soviets should renege on arms control agreements or choose to use substantial force while trying to cope with political unrest at home or along their borders. The absence of a common enemy is one dividend of success in U.S.-European relations since World War II.

The difficulty in preserving consensus increases as the United States debates its national and international goals. That debate cannot take place in isolation. Shared values, economic interdependence and common aspirations for standards of living and human rights make it essential that the United States communicate closely with its major allies.

The debate in the United States over the direction of its national and international goals is likely to intensify. Similarly, the restructuring of Europe will generate demands and policy choices that may run contrary to perceived U.S. interests and visions for the future.

United Germany has emerged as first among equals in Europe. It continues to act as a staunch ally of the United States. German policy consistently emphasizes the need for the United States to remain connected to and involved in European affairs. German support for the "Declaration Between the European Community and the United States" is a case in point (see Appendix 7).

Americans will evaluate the Germans on two principal criteria. First, there will be substantial interest in the capacity of the unified German political system to function well in both economic and security domains, while accommodating political extremes, left and right. Second, Americans will continue to view Germany as the linchpin in some form of alliance designed to prevent instability in the east from undermining the political health of the west.

The Germans will receive special scrutiny as they try to balance their eastern interests with their western political connections. American politicians can be counted on to create major disturbances if they perceive that Germany is deviating from the central course that has dominated Bonn's foreign and defense policies.

Unified Germany is expected to be a leader in Europe, economically and politically. If these expectations are to be realized, the United States must be alert to Germany's visions of a new Europe and respect differences that may arise between conceptions in Washington and those in Bonn or Berlin.

Germany's inclusion in the various international organizations previously discussed provides some comfort for those concerned about political volatility in that newly unified country. German ability to portray a steady stance and responsible demeanor is essential if U.S. policymakers are to be able to regard the Germans as the good citizens their postwar behavior would suggest they are.

Preserving cordial relations between the two nations is a function not only of government activity, but also of social and commercial interaction. Business and labor leaders on both sides of the Atlantic will be important sources of insight and ideas that can invigorate policymaking.

Both united Germany and the United States have the capacity and the inclination to lead. The remarkable events since the fall of the Berlin Wall suggest that they can lead in the same direction, toward respect for human dignity, freedom and economic well-being.

Historical parallels are dangerous, but they are sometimes revealing. Certain conditions that exist in Germany today may be familiar to those who have studied the U.S. recovery from its Civil War.

One part of Germany is economically dominant, politically mature and in clear control over the direction the disadvantaged portion of that nation must take. The German states that recovered and prospered in western Europe possess a vibrant industrial base, strong financial institutions and an infrastructure that is a major asset in continuing growth. The other portion of unified Germany has an antiquated and inefficient economic base, political institutions that have been radically challenged and changed over a very short period, and an infrastructure that cries out for investment and improvement. Tensions, some of which have ideological roots and some of which stem from resentment over the costs of unification, persist.

At the end of the Civil War, the United States, deeply divided by the tragedy through which it had passed, still shared a common language and underlying connections that even a war could not destroy entirely. The North was politically superior, economically intact and prospering. Its infrastructure was largely operable and capable of carrying growth for both the North and the South in the decades to come. Deep resentments, however, did not disappear when General Lee surrendered to General Grant.

There are, however, significant differences between Germany today and the United States of a century and a quarter ago. The United States could pursue its reunification in an environment largely free of major military threats or the necessity for political dexterity of the sort that Germany faces given its location in the center of the European continent. Further, the United States could open its west at the end of the war and thereby accommodate some of its most disadvantaged and dissatisfied citizens. Resource dependence is another difference.

Such factors made decisionmaking for U.S. leaders easier and U.S. programs more affordable.

Still, the problems associated with unifying a nation in the wake of severe trauma have some similarities. Perhaps this realization can help Americans understand the difficulties faced by unified Germany. Some Germans, in turn, may see in the history of late 19th-century United States a possible parallel to the problems they face.

More than a century separates the two situations, as does an ocean. Germany is in no position to act with the autonomy that the post-Civil War U.S. government displayed. Germany is an integral part of the history, politics and economics that have led Europe to favor cooperation rather than conflict as the century closes. The United States has played a vital part in the emergence of today's Europe. It is directly and deeply interested in the success of German unification. American political leaders, business and labor leaders, scholars, and others are likely to continue generally to understand the reasons for, if not necessarily the specific direction of, Germany's efforts to achieve political stability. Competitive strains will remain and will require delicate handling on both sides of the Atlantic.

An important point is that the government in Bonn will find it necessary to adjust to a variety of factors over which it has limited control. Strains resulting from economic integration of the European Community and developments affecting Germany's eastern and western European neighbors are not the least of these problems. Similarly, the United States—the only nation today that is a military as well as an economic superpower—has global interests and domestic requirements that may at times make it impossible for Washington to take full account of Germany's priorities and national sensitivities.

Such differences and occasional frictions are to be expected among two major world nations. The key, however, is that both, in their own albeit somewhat different interests, should bear in mind the fundamental fact that the U.S.-German relationship during the 1990s and beyond is likely to be one of the most important bilateral relationships in the world. As such, it requires careful nurturing in Washington, Bonn and Berlin.

APPENDIX 1

Membership of EC, NATO, WEU, EFTA, OECD, and CSCE

Country	EC	NATO	WEU	EFTA	OECD	CSCE
Andorra						*
Australia					*	
Austria				*	*	*
Belgium	*	*	*		*	
Bulgaria						*
Canada		*			*	*
Cyprus						*
Czechoslovakia						*
Denmark	*	*			*	*
Finland				*	*	*
France	*	*	*		*	*
Germany	*	*	*		*	*
Greece	*	*			*	*
Hungary						*
Iceland		*		*	*	*
Ireland	*				*	*
Italy	*	*	*		*	*
Japan					*	
Liechtenstein				a		*
Luxembourg	*	*	*		*	*
Malta						*
Monaco						*
Netherlands	*	*	*		*	*
New Zealand					*	
Norway		*		*	*	*
Poland						*
Portugal	*	*	*		*	*
Romania						*
San Marino						*
Spain	*	*	*		*	*
Sweden				*	*	*
Switzerland				*	*	*
Turkey		*			*	*
United Kingdom	*	*	*		*	*
United States		*			*	*
USSR						*
Yugoslavia				b	*	*

(a) Liechtenstein has an association agreement with EFTA.

(b) A joint EFTA-Yugoslavia committee promotes economic cooperation on a multilateral basis between the EFTA countries and Yugoslavia.

Chronology of Economic Events Leading to Unification

1988

JANUARY
The FRG federal government announced that, with the drastic reduction in the Bundesbank profit and higher net contributions to the European Community, the FRG budget deficit might reach DM 40 billion in 1988. It had budgeted DM 29.5 billion.

FEBRUARY
In line with EC decisions, net additional payments to the EC amounted to DM 4 billion in 1988 and were scheduled to increase to DM 10 billion by 1990.

MARCH
The FRG approved the draft of the 1990 Tax Reform Act. Gross tax relief of approximately DM 40 billion was partially offset by DM 19 billion of additional tax receipts derived from the dismantling of tax concessions and the broadening of the tax base; net relief in the first year was estimated to reach DM 21 billion.

MAY
Deutsche Bank announced it would extend the Soviet Union a credit of DM 3.5 billion.

JULY
The Bundesbank raised the discount rate from 2.5 percent to 3.0 percent and the Lombard rate from 4.5 percent to 5.0 percent.

The FRG approved the draft federal budget for 1989 and the financial plan for the period 1989 to 1992. Federal expenditure in 1989 was estimated to amount to DM 288.2 billion, 4.6 percent more than the estimate for 1988, and the federal budget deficit was to be less than DM 32 billion. In the medium term, expenditure was to rise by 2.0-2.5 percent annually. After increasing to DM 37 billion in 1990, owing to the revenue shortfalls caused by the tax reform, the federal deficit was to fall to less than DM 30 billion by 1992.

AUGUST
The Bundesbank raised the interest rate on securities under repurchase agreements from 4.0 to 4.25 percent and the discount rate from 3.0 percent to 3.5 percent.

OCTOBER

A consortium of west German banks signed an agreement providing the Soviet government a DM 3 billion line of credit "to stimulate and improve its consumer goods industry."

The FRG adopted a bill to offset differences in financial strength of the various states (structural funds). Additional funds of DM 2.45 billion per annum were made available for a period of 10 years. The program was to be reviewed in 1992 and 1995.

NOVEMBER

The Bundestag adopted the 1989 federal budget with an expenditure of DM 290.3 billion (+5.4 percent) and a federal deficit of DM 27.9 billion.

1989

JANUARY

In an attempt to counteract inflationary trends and any further weakening of the DM, the Bundesbank raised the discount rate from 3.5 percent to 4.0 percent and the Lombard rate from 5.5 percent to 6.0 percent.

APRIL

The Bundesbank raised the discount rate from 4.0 percent to 4.5 percent and the Lombard rate from 6.0 percent to 6.5 percent.

The FRG announced the removal of the withholding tax, scheduled to take effect in July 1989, until EC countries agree on a common rate.

MAY

The Bundestag approved the draft on limited deregulation of the telecommunications system.

The Bundesrat adopted the Post Office and Telecommunications Reform Act scheduled to take effect in July 1989.

JUNE

The Bundesbank raised the discount rate from 4.5 percent to 5.0 percent and the Lombard rate from 6.5 percent to 7.0 percent.

JULY

The FRG approved the draft federal budget for 1990 and the financial plan for the period 1990 to 1993. Federal expenditure in 1990 was expected to increase by 3.4 percent and the federal budget deficit to reach DM 33.7 billion. In the medium term, expenditure was to increase 3.0 percent annually on average and the federal deficit to fall to DM 25.6 billion.

OCTOBER
The Bundesbank raised the discount rate from 5 percent to 6 percent and the Lombard rate from 7 percent to 8 percent.

NOVEMBER
East Germany's new Prime Minister Hans Modrow, who was endorsed by the Volkskammer on November 17, announced a sweeping program of economic and political change and held out the prospect of relations "on a new level" with the FRG.

The FRG adopted an extensive package to promote housing construction. Funds allotted for welfare housing were to be increased to DM 2 billion. A 2.5 percent cut in interest rates for a maximum of three years was made for the construction and first-time purchase of owner-occupied residential units.

DECEMBER
On December 5, east and west Germany reached agreement on the establishment of a joint fund to provide hard currency for east Germans traveling to the west.

The west German Social Democratic Party Congress met in Berlin on December 18-20 and overwhelmingly approved a platform for the 1990 general election. The program called for the creation of a confederation of the two Germanies as a first step toward a "federal state order," an end to the deployment of Soviet and U.S. troops in Europe, the creation of nuclear weapon-free zones, and the gradual reduction of the workweek in the FRG to 30 hours in order to reduce unemployment.

Soviet Foreign Minister Eduard Shevardnadze stated in a December 19 speech to the European Parliament that "the right of self-determination . . . can only be exercised in the context of other norms and principles of international law." He posed seven questions about a united Germany that dealt with its potential structure and its role and position in the international community under existing agreements.

The Bundestag adopted the 1990 federal budget with expenditures increasing by 3 percent, leaving a deficit of DM 26.9 billion.

1990

JANUARY
Lufthansa and Interflug announced on January 19 that they would establish three joint ventures, work together on a plan for a possible new international airport serving Berlin, and cooperate in the construction of airport hotels.

The third installment of the FRG three-stage tax reduction program became effective. Gross tax cuts amounted to DM 38.7 billion, with the combination of offsetting impact from the tax benefit reduction and the closing of tax loopholes reaching DM 14 billion. As a result, net tax cuts were expected to reach DM 25 billion in 1990.

The German futures exchange opened in Frankfurt on January 26. Fifty-three domestic and foreign banks participated.

In an attempt to slow the influx of GDR citizens, a new, less generous migration allowance (*Eingleiderungsgeld*) was introduced, and GDR migrants were no longer to be considered refugees.

FEBRUARY

On February 1, Modrow announced a plan for eventual German unification through the formation of a confederation with joint institutions and a gradual transfer of sovereignty to those bodies. The proposal also required the GDR and the FRG to be "militarily neutral." Later the same day, west German Chancellor Helmut Kohl, Foreign Minister Hans Dietrich Genscher and leading members of the SPD such as Horst Ehmke rejected the notion of a neutral united Germany.

On February 6, FRG Finance Minister Theo Waigel announced a supplementary budget for 1990 for the Federal Republic. It raised the new debt ceiling by DM 6.6 billion and expanded total budget expenditures for 1990 to DM 307 billion.

The FRG Cabinet decided on February 7 to seek swift replacement of east Germany's currency with the DM. It also established a "German unity" committee responsible for preparing detailed plans for the political unification of the two Germanies.

At a February 9 press conference, the President of the Federal Republic's Bureau of Statistics announced that west German trade figures had broken records in 1989 and had registered the highest rate of increase since 1980. Imports rose 15 percent over 1988, to DM 506.6 billion, while exports rose 13 percent to 641.3 billion. He noted that the trade surplus with the United States declined from DM 16.6 billion in 1988 to DM 8.4 billion in 1989. American imports rose 32 percent, he said, while exports to the United States increased only 2.1 percent.

Kohl and Modrow agreed in principle on February 13 to start work on adopting the deutsche mark as the currency of both countries. Citing the large FRG export surplus of DM 130 billion in 1989 and the country's capital export of DM 100 billion annually, Kohl maintained that redirecting a small portion of these funds to the GDR could stimulate the GDR's economy.

On February 14, U.S. President George Bush proposed an arrangement in which the two Germanies would resolve internal problems and then join the four allied powers—the United States, the United Kingdom, France, and the Soviet Union—in resolving external issues of importance. The next day, the other three major World War II allies agreed with the two Germanies on a framework for negotiating unification.

Bremen Mayor Klaus Wedemeier announced during a February 16 Bundesrat debate that his city-state had declared a one-week freeze on accepting immigrants from the GDR and eastern Europe. He said this was necessary because Bremen had no more room to accommodate them.

The joint FRG-GDR commission charged with working out concrete steps leading to economic and monetary union met for the first time on February 20.

Genscher assured the member states of the EC on February 20 that Bonn would provide the EC with complete information and consultations on the process of German unity.

Bonn approved expenditures of DM 30 billion annually over the next five years for research on the use of renewable energy sources and wind and solar energy.

The FRG promised rapid introduction of a currency union with the GDR.

Bundesbank President Karl Otto Poehl urged caution to Bonn politicians who wished to speed up the monetary and economic union of east and west Germany.

The Bundesbank's February report expressed concern over the steep rise in interest rates on capital markets.

MARCH

The Association for International Investment (whose president is former U.S. Secretary of Commerce Elliot Richardson) announced on March 13 that west German direct investments in the United States amounted to $26.9 billion in 1989, up 12.9 percent, or $3.1 billion over 1988, making it America's fifth largest foreign direct investor. American investments in the Federal Republic amounted to $22.9 billion in 1989 compared with 12.8 billion in 1988.

Kohl remarked in Brussels that other countries had taken too little notice of the fact that the influx of thousands of east Germans into the Federal Republic had created tremendous pressure for quick establishment of a currency and social union between the two German states.

The Bundestag adopted a supplementary budget for 1990 that added 2.25 percent to the growth rate of outlays and increased the projected federal deficit by DM 7 billion to DM 34 billion. Increased expenditure included additional appropriations for public sector pay as well as for requirements deriving from upheavals in eastern Europe; subsidized loans through the ERP Special Fund for the establishment and modernization of enterprises in the GDR; DM 0.4 billion to the FRG states for the construction of temporary accommodation for immigrants from the GDR and other ethnic German refugees; and raising the federal grant to Berlin by DM 0.4 billion and assistance to other eastern European countries by DM 1 billion. DM 2 billion was made available to meet additional requirements.

A three-month wait before GDR immigrants were entitled to receive social benefits was introduced, thus putting immigrants on equal footing with FRG citizens instead of in a special category.

The GATT issued a preliminary trade report stating that in 1989 the United States replaced the Federal Republic of Germany as the world's largest exporting nation. In 1989, U.S. exports were valued at $364.4 billion, while the Federal Republic's exports totaled $341.4 billion.

APRIL
East German leaders accused Kohl of betrayal and warned about the consequences of implementing a plan to exchange west German marks for east German marks at half the rate they said he initially promised.

On April 14, Genscher called for a relaxation of the strict COCOM export requirements on high-tech products to eastern Europe. He noted that "it is in our interest that the GDR and the states of central and eastern Europe are able to increase their productivity through access to the latest technological developments."

East German Prime Minister Lothar de Maizière announced a plan for economic and social union with west Germany by July 1, 1990.

The FRG announced its agreement to convert ostmarks to deutsche marks at a 1:1 exchange rate.

The FRG and GDR governments agreed to establish an economic, monetary and social union by summer 1990.

MAY
The FRG Metalworkers Union and the Metal Employers' Association reached an agreement on a new contract that called for a 6 percent pay increase and a reduction of the workweek from the present 37 hours to 36 hours on April 1, 1993, and to 35 hours on October 1, 1995.

Kohl said he was receptive to the idea of holding all-German elections in late 1990.

The treaty to create a monetary, economic and social union between the FRG and the GDR as of July 2, 1990, was signed by the two governments on May 18.

The FRG and GDR governments agreed on monetary conversion provisions: conversion at a 1:1 rate of cash and saving accounts up to amounts of OM 6,000 for people 59 and older, OM 4,000 for those 15 to 58 and OM 2,000 for those 14 and younger. Most other financial assets and liabilities were to be exchanged at an OM/DM rate of 2:1. Wages, salaries, housing rents, pensions, and other contractual current income payments were initially to be converted at 1:1. In the case of earnings, the reference level was that of May 1, 1990; for social security pensions, the base for benefit entitlements and contributions was to be changed to that of the Federal Republic.

The west German SPD announced its opposition to the treaty for German economic unification.

Walter Wallmann, Minister President of the west German state of Hesse, stated that, although some U.S. troops should remain in the FRG, bases in major urban areas should be abandoned.

Chancellor candidate Oskar Lafontaine stated that the SPD should vote against the economic unification treaty.

JUNE
Kohl, in a commencement address at Harvard University, spoke of his vision of a "United States of Europe," open to any who wished to join.

The Currency Union Treaty was ratified by the Bundestag.

The Currency Union Treaty was ratified by the Bundesrat.

JULY
Currency union was formalized between the GDR and the FRG.

The nations of the European Community began the first formal stage of the process leading toward economic and monetary union (EMU).

Kohl agreed to limit the troop strength of a united Germany to 370,000.

AUGUST
The FRG and the GDR signed an election treaty that established rules for an all-German election on December 2, 1990.

On August 23, the People's Chamber in the Volkskammer resolved to accede to the FRG on October 3, 1990.

The Bavarian Christian Social Union called for a halt to all new monetary assistance for east Germany.

SEPTEMBER
The Treaty on the Final Settlement with Respect to Germany (2+4 Treaty) was signed on September 12.

The GDR Volkskammer and the FRG Bundestag ratified the unification treaty.

At the annual meeting of the IMF and the World Bank on September 26, Poehl announced that the bank would not relax its strict anti-inflation policy.

OCTOBER
The document suspending rights of the four victorious parties of World War II (Britain, France, the Soviet Union, and the United States) over Germany was signed in New York.

October 3 was German unification day.

The Federal Labor Agency in Nuremberg announced that unemployment in the eastern part of Germany rose by 83,500 to reach a total of 444,825, a rate of 5 percent, since monetary union. The agency also reported that the number of people working reduced hours totaled 1,771,576 in mid-September.

British Chancellor of the Exchequer John Major announced full British membership in the European Monetary System.

Elections to the FRG state parliaments were held in the five states of the former GDR and in Bavaria.

The summit meeting of the leaders of the European Community closed with an agreement to put the second phase of the economic and currency union into effect on January 1, 1994. The U.K. objected to the agreement.

The Bundestag passed its third supplementary budget for 1990, containing spending increases of DM 20.2 billion to a total of DM 396.1 billion.

NOVEMBER
The Bundesbank raised the Lombard rate from 8.0 percent to 8.5 percent. The discount rate remained at 6.0 percent.

The European Community held a summit of heads of state and government in Rome on November 3. A statement endorsing German unification was passed unanimously.

The council of economic experts that advises the German federal government called for a more consistently tight monetary policy in its annual report on the state of the German economy.

Kohl called on western German businesses to invest in the east, saying that only a massive investment push could create an economic upswing there.

DECEMBER

Coalition talks between the CDU, the CSU and the FDP began after
the December 2 election. They focused extensively on tax issues.

The number of unemployed people in western Germany rose by 99,000
in December, increasing the annual rate from 6.4 percent to 6.8 percent.

The number of unemployed people in eastern Germany rose by 53,000
in December to a total of 642,000. The unemployment rate increased
from 6.7 to 7.3 percent. The number of short-time workers increased to
1,795,000.

APPENDIX 3

Chronology of Political Events Leading to Unification

1988

JANUARY

Franz Joseph Strauss, head of the Bavarian Christian Social Union, visited Moscow and met with senior Soviet officials. He stated that he was "deeply convinced of the honesty of the will to change and the sincerity of joint objectives."

1989

JANUARY

In Leipzig, GDR police detained 80 protestors who demanded freedom of expression and assembly.

East German President Erich Honecker announced that the GDR would reduce its armed forces by 10,000 (to roughly 125,000) and cut military spending 10 percent.

MAY

Nationwide communal elections were held in the GDR on May 7. The validity of their results was challenged by a group of east German church leaders who alleged widespread falsifications. The lists of unopposed candidates produced a 98.77 percent turnout with a favorable vote of 98.85 percent.

In Leipzig, GDR, a May 7 demonstration by approximately 1,000 people called for a democratic, multicandidate electoral system.

JUNE

U.S. President George Bush called on the Soviet Union and its allies to end the division of Europe and offered a four-point plan for European reunification in a speech in Mainz, FRG. He proposed free elections and political pluralism in eastern Europe, demolition of the Berlin Wall, joint east-west efforts on common environmental problems, and reduction of conventional forces in Europe.

Troops attacked unarmed students protesting in Beijing's Tiananmen Square on June 3-4. Western sources reported that between 2,000 and 5,000 civilians and soldiers were killed. Official Chinese reports put the death toll at approximately "300 counterrevolutionaries."

In Bonn on June 12, FRG Chancellor Helmut Kohl and Soviet President Mikhail Gorbachev signed a joint political declaration on human rights and economic and environmental cooperation.

Gorbachev stated that the Berlin Wall was not necessarily permanent and that it would be taken down when the conditions that created it no longer existed.

Gorbachev stated on June 15 that he could not believe the intentions of the Chinese students demonstrating in Tiananmen Square had been "evil."

AUGUST
West Germany closed its mission in east Berlin to slow the flow of east Germans seeking to emigrate.

East German border guards who deserted to the west stated that east Berlin had ordered border guards not to shoot at escaping civilians except in self-defense.

West Germany closed its embassy in Budapest because it was filled with more than 180 east Germans trying to emigrate.

SEPTEMBER
In Leipzig on September 4, police violently dispersed several hundred demonstrators who were protesting against political and social problems in the GDR. Similar demonstrations took place on September 11 and 18 with similar results.

Fifty thousand east Germans fled through Hungary. Kohl expressed gratitude to the Hungarian government for granting safe passage. Czechoslovakia allowed 6,000 more east Germans to flee.

A Soviet Politburo member accused west Germany of encouraging the departure of approximately 10,000 east Germans in two days.

East Germany sent a formal diplomatic note to Hungary stating that "Hungary's behavior was a clear violation of legal treaties and thus constituted a violation of the basic interests of the GDR."

Gorbachev announced that he would visit east Berlin on October 7 for the 40th anniversary of the GDR.

The New Forum, an umbrella organization designed to coordinate the activities of independent, informal political groups, was the first and largest of several new groups formed to campaign for change in east Germany. It applied for official permission to field candidates in the GDR parliamentary election in May 1990.

The GDR government declared the New Forum pro-democracy group illegal and accused the group's organizers of "anti-state policies" and attempting to deceive the public about its true intentions.

Approximately 8,000 people marched through Leipzig calling for democracy. Police did not interfere.

OCTOBER

West German Foreign Minister Hans Dietrich Genscher and GDR authorities agreed to allow the transportation of east German refugees from FRG embassies in Prague and Warsaw.

Valentin M. Falin, advisor to Gorbachev, said that the GDR made the right decision in allowing east Germans in Prague and Warsaw to emigrate to the west.

East Germany allowed up to 11,000 east Germans in Prague to travel to the FRG via the GDR in trains and trucks.

East Germany closed its border with Czechoslovakia.

Gorbachev arrived in the GDR and declared that Moscow would not interfere in its problems.

Protestors clashed with police and security forces throughout east Germany during the GDR's 40th anniversary celebration.

The GDR Politburo cited a need to explore the refugee exodus to the west.

More than 100,000 demonstrators demanding reforms marched in Leipzig. It was the largest demonstration since the 1953 east German uprising.

Honecker was ousted. He was replaced by Egon Krenz.

Krenz met with east German senior church leaders, to whom he pledged a "new chapter of constructive cooperation."

Bush, commenting on pressure for political reform in east Germany, said that he believed change was "inexorable" and that he did not share the worries of some European leaders about possible German reunification.

The GDR Parliament elected Krenz President.

In Leipzig, 300,000 east Germans marched. They demanded free elections, elimination of the secret police and legalization of the New Forum opposition movement.

NOVEMBER

East Germany lifted the ban on travel to Czechoslovakia; as many as 8,000 east Germans crossed the border within hours.

Two days after conferring with Gorbachev in Moscow, Krenz returned home and asked his citizens to stop fleeing the country. He promised far-reaching reforms and dismissed five senior Politburo members.

In east Berlin, 500,000 east Germans protested in favor of political change.

The GDR Cabinet resigned.

On November 7, the GDR Politburo resigned and a new one was elected. The four new full members elected were Hans Modrow, Wolfgang Herger, Wolfgang Rauchfuss, and Gerhard Schuerer.

The New Forum was legalized after November 8 discussions between New Forum and Communist Party (SED) leaders.

Kohl, in his state of the nation speech before the FRG Parliament, promised "comprehensive aid" for east Germany if it held free elections and made fundamental changes in its state-planned economy.

The Berlin Wall opened on November 9, 1989.

The Soviet Union praised changes affecting the Communist Party in the GDR and reiterated its nonintervention policy.

The east German Christian Democratic Union (CDU Ost) elected Lothar de Maizière its new chairman.

The Soviet Union welcomed the GDR's opening of the Berlin Wall as a positive move, but emphasized that east Germany's borders would be inviolable until radical changes were made in east and west military alliances.

During the weekend of November 19, 3 million east Germans visited the Federal Republic. Most returned to the GDR.

Gorbachev stated that German unification was not under discussion.

East Germany's new Prime Minister Hans Modrow, who was endorsed by the Volkskammer on November 17, announced a sweeping program of economic and political change and held out the prospect of relations "on a new level" with the FRG.

Kohl presented a "10-point plan" to Parliament designed to lead to the eventual unification of the two German states.

Prominent east German artists and intellectuals issued a petition titled "For Our Country." It advocated the continuing development of the GDR as a socialist alternative to the FRG. Krenz signed the petition.

The FRG adopted an extensive package to promote housing construction. Funds allotted for welfare housing were to be increased to DM 2 billion. A 2.5 percent cut in interest rates for a maximum of three years was made for the construction and first-time purchase of owner-occupied residential units.

DECEMBER
On December 1, the Volkskammer voted 420 to 0, with 5 abstentions, to remove the SED's constitutionally guaranteed "leading role" in the GDR government.

East German Communist Party leadership under Krenz collapsed, and the GDR's entire Politburo and Central Committee resigned on December 3.

On December 5, east and west Germany reached agreement on the establishment of a joint fund to provide hard currency for east Germans traveling to the west.

Honecker and top members of his former government were placed under house arrest.

Krenz resigned as Chairman of the GDR Council of State and Chairman of the National Defense Council on December 6.

Gorbachev stated that the division of Germany into two states at the end of World War II had provided an element of stability in Europe. "Any artificial prodding and pushing of [the German unity] question . . . could only make the processes taking place more difficult."

French President Francois Mitterrand stated that "none of the countries in Europe can afford to act without considering the others [and the] historical situation." He noted that this situation meant that the German people and their governments would have to take into account the opinions of other European countries on reunification.

Round-table discussions were held between GDR government, church and opposition leaders.

The GDR Communist Party elected Gregor Gysi chairman.

At the request of the Soviet Union, ambassadors of the four victorious World War II powers met in Berlin for the first time since the signing of the Four-Power Agreement on Berlin in 1971.

The New Forum formally constituted itself as a political party.

At its December 16-17 session, an emergency SED party congress changed the party name from SED to SED-PDS (Sozialistiche Einheitspartei Deutschlands-Partei des Demokratischen Sozialismus).

The FRG Social Democratic Party Congress met in Berlin on December 18-20 and overwhelmingly approved a platform for the 1990 general election. The program called for the creation of a confederation of the two Germanies as a first step toward a "federal state order," an end to the deployment of Soviet and U.S. troops in Europe, the creation of nuclear weapon-free zones, and the gradual reduction of the workweek in the FRG to 30 hours in order to reduce unemployment.

Soviet Foreign Minister Eduard Shevardnadze stated in a December 19 speech to the European Parliament that "the right of self-determination . . . can only be exercised in the context of other norms and principles of international law." He posed seven questions about a united Germany that dealt with its potential structure and its role and position in the international community under existing agreements.

Mitterrand visited east Germany on December 20-22 and commented that "German unity is first and foremost for Germans. France would not stand in the way, but the German people must take the European balance into account in its decisions."

The FRG and GDR governments agreed to form a common monetary fund to assist GDR citizens traveling to the FRG.

1990

JANUARY
Lufthansa and Interflug announced on January 19 that they would establish three joint ventures, work together on a plan for a possible new international airport serving Berlin, and cooperate in the construction of airport hotels.

On January 28, agreement was reached at GDR "round-table talks" between the government and opposition groups to form an all-party government of national responsibility that would hold office until the election date of March 18.

The FRG Social Democrats won 54.4 percent of the vote in elections for the Saarland state parliament on January 28. The SPD expanded its representation in the 51-seat state legislature from 26 to 30 seats.

According to Modrow, Gorbachev stated that a single Germany "is not ruled out in the future."

In an attempt to slow the influx of GDR citizens, a new, less generous migration allowance (*Eingleiderungsgeld*) was introduced, and GDR migrants were no longer to be considered refugees.

FEBRUARY

On February 1, Modrow announced a plan for eventual German unification through the formation of a confederation with joint institutions and a gradual transfer of sovereignty to those bodies. The proposal also required the GDR and the FRG to be "militarily neutral." Later the same day, Kohl, Genscher and leading members of the SPD such as Horst Ehmke rejected the notion of a neutral united Germany.

On February 6, FRG Finance Minister Theo Waigel announced a supplementary budget for 1990. It raised the new debt ceiling by DM 6.6 billion and expanded total budget expenditures for 1990 to DM 307 billion.

The FRG Cabinet decided on February 7 to seek swift replacement of east Germany's currency with the DM. It also established a "German unity" committee responsible for preparing detailed plans for the political unification of the two Germanies.

Alexander Yakovlev, a key political ally of Gorbachev, said on February 7 that Soviet security "must be very firmly guaranteed" in any new arrangement between east and west Germany.

Bush said on February 7 that a united Germany should "remain tied to NATO in some way" although NATO itself might undergo a change.

Kohl said he and Gorbachev agreed that the issue of German unification was up to "the German people alone."

Kohl and Modrow agreed in principle on February 13 to start work on adopting the deutsche mark as the currency of both countries. Citing the large FRG export surplus of DM 130 billion in 1989 and the country's capital export of DM 100 billion annually, Kohl maintained that redirecting a small portion of these funds to the GDR could stimulate the GDR's economy.

Shevardnadze, when asked whether the Soviet Union could accept a unified Germany, simply shrugged.

On February 14, Bush proposed an arrangement in which the two Germanies would resolve internal problems and then join the four allied powers—the United States, the United Kingdom, France, and the Soviet Union—in resolving external issues of importance. The next day, the other three major World War II allies agreed with the two Germanies on a framework for negotiating unification.

In a policy statement on February 15 in Paris, Kohl reaffirmed the Federal Republic's stance against any attempts to go it alone. He stressed that Germany must remain anchored in a NATO that would concentrate on its political role.

Bremen Mayor Klaus Wedemeier announced during a February 16 Bundesrat debate that his city-state had declared a one-week freeze on accepting immigrants from the GDR and eastern Europe. He said this was necessary because Bremen had no more room to accommodate them.

Shevardnadze said on February 20 that German unification would proceed much more slowly than west Germany expected. The Bonn government immediately disputed the truth of his statement.

The joint FRG-GDR commission charged with working out concrete steps leading to economic and monetary union met for the first time on February 20.

Genscher assured the member states of the EC on February 20 that Bonn would provide the EC with complete information and consultations on the process of German unity.

Kohl made his first election campaign appearance in the east German town of Erfurt on behalf of the "Alliance for Democracy." Approximately 130,000 attended the rally.

Pressure mounted quickly for Kohl to clarify Germany's position on the Polish border question.

Bush and Kohl agreed at Camp David that a united Germany must remain "a full member of NATO, including participation in the military structure," and that U.S. troops should remain stationed in a united Germany as a "continued guarantor for stability."

Several leading U.S. senators complained to Bush that Kohl's refusal to forswear unequivocally any German claims to Polish territory was unacceptable.

The FRG promised rapid introduction of a currency union with the GDR.

Bundesbank President Karl Otto Poehl urged caution to Bonn politicians who wished to speed up the monetary and economic union of east and west Germany.

MARCH
Genscher differed publicly with Kohl over the government's position on the German-Polish border question.

Gorbachev stated that NATO membership was "absolutely out of the question" for a united Germany.

The FRG coalition government reached an agreement on a proposal under which west German and east German parliaments would adopt identical resolutions renouncing any territorial claims to Poland and would direct a future, unified Germany to put its "final seal" on the issue.

On March 8, Kohl stated that the unification process was moving quickly because of uncontrollable events, not because of encouragement from his government.

Mitterrand, on March 9, clearly endorsed the Polish position that existing borders with its neighbors should not be changed.

Kohl assured his neighbors and allies on March 12 that German unification would not occur until 1991.

In Bonn, preliminary talks on German unification began between the two Germanies and the four World War II allies.

In GDR elections on March 18, the Christian Democratic Alliance, a conservative coalition of parties, won a substantial victory, with 48.2 percent of the vote and 193 seats in the 400-seat GDR parliament.

Oskar Lafontaine was named SPD candidate for Chancellor in the December FRG elections.

The Bush Administration cited the Christian Democratic Alliance victory in the GDR as support for an inexorable march toward unification. The United States also expressed its hope that a united Germany would remain in NATO.

The Soviet Union said that "the massive interference" of west German political parties in east German elections had influenced the result of the GDR elections, and it cautioned against accelerating the pace of unification.

Kohl remarked in Brussels that other countries had taken too little notice of the fact that the influx of thousands of east Germans into the Federal Republic had created tremendous pressure for quick establishment of a currency and social union between the two German states.

A three-month wait before GDR immigrants became entitled to receive social benefits was introduced, thus putting immigrants on equal footing with FRG citizens instead of in a special category.

APRIL

East German leaders accused Kohl of betrayal and warned about the consequences of implementing a plan to exchange west German marks for east German marks at half the rate they said he initially promised.

The United States and the Federal Republic rejected a Soviet proposal that a united Germany temporarily remain a member of both NATO and the Warsaw Pact.

The removal of U.S. cruise missiles from west Germany began (in accordance with the 1987 INF Treaty).

On April 14, Genscher called for a relaxation of the strict COCOM export requirements on high-tech products to eastern Europe. He noted that "it is in our interest that the GDR and the states of central and eastern Europe are able to increase their productivity through access to the latest technological developments."

De Maizière announced a plan for economic and social union with west Germany by July 1, 1990.

The FRG announced its agreement to convert ostmarks to deutsche marks at a 1:1 exchange rate.

Oskar Lafontaine was seriously injured when a woman stabbed him at a campaign rally.

The east German leadership announced that, despite objections from the USSR, it would be willing to become part of a "changed" NATO following unification.

The FRG and GDR governments agreed to establish an economic, monetary and social union by summer 1990.

MAY

U.S. Defense Secretary Richard Cheney said that the United States should keep a strong military presence in west Germany until the USSR removes its nuclear forces from east Germany.

Local elections were held in east Germany on May 6. All major parties in west Germany publicly expressed satisfaction with the results.

U.S. Secretary of State James Baker traveled to Poland to reassure Polish leaders that a unified Germany would pose no threat to their nation and to invite Poland to join part of the discussions on unification.

State elections were held May 13 in North Rhine-Westphalia and Lower Saxony. The SPD improved its previous showing in both elections, polling a majority 50.6 percent of the votes in North Rhine-Westphalia while the CDU polled 36.7 percent, a 0.2 percent increase.

In Lower Saxony the SPD polled 44.3 percent and the CDU 42.2 percent. The balance in the Bundesrat thus switched from a CDU-CSU majority to a 27-18 majority in favor of the SPD, which included 4 limited Berlin votes.

On May 14, political negotiations on the unification treaty began in Berlin.

Kohl said he was receptive to the idea of holding all-German elections in late 1990.

On May 17, Sir Leon Brittan, Vice President of the European Commission, proposed setting up a European Security Community alongside Euratom and ECSC. It would subsume NATO's Eurogroup, which he described as lacking overall strategy.

The treaty creating a monetary, economic and social union between the FRG and the GDR as of July 2, 1990, was signed by the two governments on May 18.

The FRG and GDR governments agreed on monetary conversion provisions: conversion at a 1:1 rate of cash and saving accounts up to amounts of OM 6,000 for people 59 and older, OM 4,000 for those 15 to 58 and OM 2,000 for those 14 and younger. Most other financial assets and liabilities were to be exchanged at an OM/DM rate of 2:1. Wages, salaries, housing rents, pensions, and other contractual current income payments were initially to be converted at 1:1. In the case of earnings, the reference level was that of May 1, 1990; for social security pensions, the base for benefit entitlements and contributions was to be changed to that of the Federal Republic.

The west German SPD announced its opposition to the treaty for German economic unification.

Walter Wallmann, Minister President of the west German state of Hesse, stated that although some U.S. troops should remain in the FRG, bases in major urban areas should be abandoned.

On May 26, Gorbachev announced that the USSR would review its priorities on European arms agreements if a united Germany joined NATO.

Lafontaine stated that the SPD should vote against the economic unification treaty.

Gorbachev strongly urged the west not to attempt to impose a European security framework in which a unified Germany would be part of NATO. However, he said that "certain ideas and suggestions" had been put forward for breaking the impasse on a united Germany's military status and that the principal parties would study the matter further.

JUNE
Kohl, in a commencement address at Harvard University, spoke of his vision of a "United States of Europe," open to any who wished to join.

Shevardnadze and Genscher stated that they had made progress in tackling key obstacles in the path of German unification.

Gorbachev announced for the first time that he could envision west German soldiers remaining in NATO without a parallel role for east German forces in the Warsaw Pact.

The Currency Union Treaty was ratified by the Bundestag.

The Currency Union Treaty was ratified by the Bundesrat.

JULY
Currency union was formalized between the GDR and the FRG.

The nations of the European Community began the first formal stage of the process leading to economic and monetary union (EMU).

Gorbachev and Kohl announced their agreement that united Germany must become a full member of NATO.

Kohl agreed to limit the troop strength of a united Germany to 370,000.

Kohl confirmed the date for the all-German parliamentary elections was likely to be December 2, 1990.

The Polish border issue was reconciled at the 2+4 talks when both Germanies agreed that a united Germany would in "the shortest possible time" complete a treaty guaranteeing Poland's existing borders.

AUGUST
The FRG and the GDR signed an election treaty that established the rules for an all-German election on December 2, 1990.

De Maizière proposed moving all-German elections to October 14.

On August 23, the People's Chamber in the Volkskammer resolved to accede to the FRG on October 3, 1990.

The Free Democratic Party united its western and eastern halves.

The Bavarian Christian Social Union called for a halt to all new monetary assistance for east Germany.

The east German Social Democrats quit the coalition government there.

SEPTEMBER
The Treaty on the Final Settlement with Respect to Germany (2+4 Treaty) was signed on September 12.

The GDR Volkskammer and the FRG Bundestag ratified the unification treaty.

The United States announced withdrawal of 60,000 U.S. troops and the closing of several U.S.-operated installations in Germany over the next few years. Bonn welcomed the announcement.

The FRG constitutional court ruled that extending the FRG electoral rules for representation in the Bundestag to the whole of Germany contravened the principle of equal chances for the parties. Parties must garner at least 5 percent of the vote in national elections or carry three electoral districts to seat representatives in the Bundestag.

OCTOBER
The document suspending rights of the four victorious parties of World War II (Britain, France, the Soviet Union, and the United States) over Germany was signed in New York.

CSCE foreign ministers began a two-day meeting in New York to lay the groundwork for November's summit meeting of the CSCE.

Kohl announced that five politicians from the former GDR would be members of his cabinet without portfolio: former President of the People's Chamber Sabine Bergmann-Pohl, former Prime Minister Lothar de Maizière, former State Secretary Guenther Krause, Free Democratic Party leader Rainer Ortleb, and Chairperson of the Christian Social Party Hansjoachim Walther. One hundred forty-four representatives from the former GDR would be seated in the Bundestag, bringing the total to 663.

On October 2, the FRG and GDR Christian Democratic Parties merged to form the first all-German Christian Democratic Party since 1946. Kohl was elected party leader, and de Maizière was elected his deputy.

October 3 was German unification day.

One hundred forty-four deputies from the eastern states were seated in the Bundestag. This increased the number of Bundestag deputies from 519 to 663. The CDU/CSU party group in the Bundestag increased from 234 to 305 deputies, the SPD from 193 to 226, the FDP from 48 to 57, and the Green Party/Alliance '90 from 42 to 49. The PDS seated 24 members.

The CDU won the most votes in four of the five eastern states that held elections on October 14 and obtained an absolute majority in Saxony.

(continued)

The SPD was the clear winner in Brandenburg. The CSU maintained a majority in Bavaria.

The Federal Labor Agency in Nuremberg announced that unemployment in the eastern part of Germany rose by 83,500 to reach a total of 444,825, a rate of 5 percent, since monetary union. The agency also reported that the number of people working reduced hours totaled 1,771,576 in mid-September.

The PDS headquarters in Berlin were searched on October 19 without a search warrant. Police sought evidence of misappropriated funds that allegedly were illegally transferred from SED (the former PDS or Communist Party) accounts.

British Chancellor of the Exchequer John Major announced full British membership in the European Monetary System.

The Bundestag voted to approve a treaty between the FRG and the USSR regulating the stationing and withdrawal of Soviet troops from eastern Germany. Part of the treaty ensures German financial support while troops remain in the east. The government estimated the cost would be DM 13 billion.

NOVEMBER
The Bundesbank raised the Lombard rate from 8 percent to 8.5 percent. The discount rate remained at 6 percent.

The Institute for Small-to-Medium-Sized Businesses (Bonn) estimated that 120,000 new businesses were founded in eastern Germany in the first nine months of 1990.

The European Community held a summit of heads of state and government in Rome on November 3. A statement endorsing German unification was passed unanimously.

Gorbachev visited Bonn beginning November 9. He and Kohl signed three treaties. The first was a general treaty of friendship and cooperation; the second set out specific economic cooperation; and the third provided for cooperation between labor and social service agencies.

Genscher and Polish Foreign Minister Krzysztof Skubiszewski signed the German-Polish border treaty in Warsaw on November 14.

Kohl called on western German businesses to invest in the east, saying that only a massive investment push could create an economic upswing there.

Following a confrontation between police and squatters in Berlin, the "Red-Green" coalition government of Berlin collapsed when the Alternative List (Green) Party voted for a breakup. The Social

Democrats and the Alternative List Party had governed Berlin (west) since March 1989.

Bush visited Kohl and discussed the upcoming Conference on Security and Cooperation in Europe meeting as well as the crisis in the Persian Gulf.

The CSCE conference in Paris on November 19-21 finished signing the "Paris Charter for a New Europe: A New Age of Democracy." Among the provisions was the first CSCE organization in Vienna, the Center for Conflict Resolution. A secretariat for the CSCE is to be established in Prague. Troop ceilings for NATO and the Warsaw Pact forces, agreed to in principle in October in preparatory CSCE meetings, were endorsed. The Vienna negotiations on conventional forces were projected to continue until 1992. Increased cooperation on European security matters was called for.

At the same time as the CSCE Paris meeting, a *TransAtlantic Declaration* was signed between the United States and Europe and between Canada and Europe. This document acknowledged the deep transatlantic ties and pledged the signatories to safeguard peace, promote open trade and meet semiannually at the highest levels to consult on common interests. Genscher said that this agreement as well as the CSCE would cement America's role as a "partner in the new European order."

Kohl asked Germans to send food and other aid to the USSR. By the end of November, nearly DM 900 million had been collected.

The German interior ministry announced that roughly 25,000 eastern Germans had moved west each month since the July currency union. Before the March 18 elections in the GDR, approximately 10,000 GDR citizens had come west each week.

DECEMBER
The first all-German elections in almost 60 years took place on December 2, 1990. The ruling coalition of CDU/CSU and the FDP won enough votes to remain in power. The SPD made a poorer showing than it had in the 1987 election. The Green Party in the west did not garner enough votes to break the 5 percent barrier. But because of the separate 5 percent barrier in the east and west, the Alliance '90/Green Party from the east was represented. The Party of Democratic Socialism (SED, the former east German communists) also won representation in the Bundestag.

Coalition talks between the CDU, the CSU and the FDP began after the December 2 election. They focused extensively on tax issues.

The Uruguay Round of the GATT negotiations was broken off on December 7, largely because of an inability to reach agreement on agricultural issues.

Kohl and Mitterrand put forward proposals on how to foster European political union. Their major proposal was to initiate majority votes on all issues before the European Council. They also proposed strengthening the European Parliament and European cooperation on defense matters.

On December 15, the European Council held a summit to begin consultations on European political union and to continue consultations on European economic and monetary union. At the summit, leaders decided to establish an ongoing Inter-governmental Conference to discuss, among other items, expanding EC scope in matters of foreign and defense policy. A continued role for NATO and closer cooperation between the EC and the WEU were discussed. The Italian plan for merger of the latter two institutions was not endorsed.

APPENDIX 4

Chronology of Security
Events Leading to Unification

1988

JANUARY
Franz Joseph Strauss, head of the Bavarian Christian Social Union, visited Moscow and met with senior Soviet officials. He stated that he was "deeply convinced of the honesty of the will to change and the sincerity of joint objectives."

1989

JANUARY
East German President Erich Honecker announced that the GDR would reduce its armed forces by 10,000 (to roughly 125,000) and cut military spending 10 percent.

JUNE
U.S. President George Bush called on the Soviet Union and its allies to end the division of Europe and offered a four-point plan for European reunification in a speech in Mainz, FRG. He proposed free elections and political pluralism in eastern Europe, demolition of the Berlin Wall, joint east-west efforts on common environmental problems, and reduction of conventional forces in Europe.

JULY
East German refugees occupied FRG missions in east Berlin, Budapest and Prague.

SEPTEMBER
Fifty thousand east Germans fled through Hungary. FRG Chancellor Helmut Kohl expressed gratitude to the Hungarian government for granting safe passage. Czechoslovakia allowed 6,000 more east Germans to flee.

OCTOBER
Honecker was ousted from office and replaced by Egon Krenz.

Bush, commenting on pressure for political reform in east Germany, said that he believed change was "inexorable" and that he did not share the worries of some European leaders about possible German reunification.

NOVEMBER

The Berlin Wall opened on November 9, 1989.

The Soviet Union welcomed the GDR's opening of the Berlin Wall as a positive move, but emphasized that east Germany's borders would remain inviolable until radical changes were made in east and west military alliances.

DECEMBER

Soviet President Mikhail Gorbachev stated that the division of Germany into two states at the end of World War II had provided an element of stability in Europe. "Any artificial prodding and pushing of [the German unity] question . . . could only make the processes taking place more difficult."

French President Francois Mitterrand stated that "none of the countries in Europe can afford to act without considering the others [and the] historical situation." He noted that this situation meant that the German people and their governments would have to take into account the opinions of other European countries on reunification.

At the request of the Soviet Union, ambassadors of the four victorious World War II powers met in Berlin for the first time since the signing of the Four-Power Agreement on Berlin in 1971.

The FRG Social Democratic Party Congress met in Berlin on December 18-20 and overwhelmingly approved a platform for the 1990 general election. The program called for the creation of a confederation of the two Germanies as a first step toward a "federal state order," an end to the deployment of Soviet and U.S. troops in Europe, the creation of nuclear weapon-free zones, and the gradual reduction of the workweek in the FRG to 30 hours in order to reduce unemployment.

Soviet Foreign Minister Eduard Shevardnadze stated in a December 19 speech to the European Parliament that "the right of self-determination . . . can only be exercised in the context of other norms and principles of international law." He posed seven questions about a united Germany that dealt with its potential structure and its role and position in the international community under existing agreements.

Mitterrand visited east Germany on December 20-22 and commented that "German unity is first and foremost for Germans. France would not stand in the way, but the German people must take the European balance into account in its decisions."

1990

JANUARY

According to GDR Prime Minister Hans Modrow, Gorbachev stated that a single Germany "is not ruled out in the future."

FEBRUARY

On February 1, Modrow announced a plan for eventual German unification through the formation of a confederation with joint institutions and a gradual transfer of sovereignty to those bodies. The proposal also required the GDR and the FRG to be "militarily neutral." Later the same day, Kohl, west German Foreign Minister Hans Dietrich Genscher and leading members of the SPD such as Horst Ehmke rejected the notion of a neutral united Germany.

Alexander Yakovlev, a key political ally of Gorbachev, said on February 7 that Soviet security "must be very firmly guaranteed" in any new arrangement between east and west Germany.

Bush said on February 7 that a united Germany should "remain tied to NATO in some way" although NATO itself might undergo a change.

Kohl said he and Gorbachev agreed that the issue of German unification was up to "the German people alone."

Shevardnadze, when asked whether the Soviet Union could accept a unified Germany, simply shrugged.

On February 14, Bush proposed an arrangement in which the two Germanies would resolve internal problems and then join the four allied powers (the United States, the United Kingdom, France, and the Soviet Union) in resolving external issues of importance. The next day, the other three major World War II allies agreed with the two Germanies on a framework for negotiating unification.

In a policy statement on February 15 in Paris, Kohl reaffirmed the Federal Republic's position against any attempts to go it alone. He stressed that Germany must remain anchored in a NATO that would concentrate on its political role.

Shevardnadze said on February 20 that German unification would proceed much more slowly than west Germany expected. The Bonn government immediately disputed the truth of his statement.

Pressure mounted quickly for Kohl to clarify Germany's position on the Polish border question.

Bush and Kohl agreed at Camp David that a united Germany must remain "a full member of NATO, including participation in the military structure," and that U.S. troops should remain stationed in a united Germany as a "continued guarantor for stability."

Several leading U.S. senators complained to Bush that Kohl's refusal to forswear unequivocally any German claims to Polish territory was unacceptable.

MARCH
Genscher differed publicly with Kohl over the government's position on the German-Polish border question.

Gorbachev stated that NATO membership was "absolutely out of the question" for a united Germany.

The FRG coalition government reached an agreement on a proposal under which west German and east German parliaments would adopt identical resolutions renouncing any territorial claims to Poland and would direct a future, unified Germany to put its "final seal" on the issue.

Mitterrand, on March 9, clearly endorsed the Polish position that existing borders with its neighbors should remain.

In Bonn, preliminary talks on German unification began between the two Germanies and the four World War II allies.

Conservatives dominated the first free east German election on March 18.

The Bush Administration cited the Christian Democratic Alliance victory in the GDR as support for an inexorable march toward unification. The United States also expressed its hope that a united Germany would remain in NATO.

The Soviet Union said that "the massive interference" of west German political parties in east German elections had influenced the result of the GDR elections, and it cautioned against accelerating the pace of unification.

APRIL
The United States and the Federal Republic rejected a Soviet proposal that a united Germany temporarily remain a member of both NATO and the Warsaw Pact.

The removal of U.S. cruise missiles from west Germany began (in accordance with the 1987 INF Treaty).

On April 14, Genscher called for a relaxation of the strict COCOM export requirements on high-tech products to eastern Europe. He noted that "it is in our interest that the GDR and the states of central and eastern Europe are able to increase their productivity through access to the latest technological developments."

The east German leadership announced that despite objections from the USSR, it would be willing to become part of a "changed" NATO following unification.

The FRG and GDR governments agreed to establish an economic, monetary and social union by summer 1990.

MAY
U.S. Defense Secretary Richard Cheney said that the United States should keep a strong military presence in west Germany until the USSR removes its nuclear forces from east Germany.

Secretary of State James Baker traveled to Poland to assure Polish leaders that a unified Germany would pose no threat to their nation and to invite Poland to join part of the discussions on unification.

On May 14, political negotiations on the unification treaty began in Berlin.

Kohl said that he was receptive to the idea of holding all-German elections in late 1990.

On May 17, Sir Leon Brittan, Vice President of the European Commission, proposed setting up a European Security Community alongside Euratom and ECSC. It would subsume NATO's Eurogroup, which he described as lacking overall strategy.

The treaty creating a monetary, economic and social union between the FRG and the GDR as of July 2, 1990, was signed by the two governments on May 18.

Walter Wallmann, Minister President of the west German state of Hesse, stated that although some U.S. troops should remain in the FRG, bases in urban areas should be abandoned.

On May 26, Gorbachev announced that the USSR would review its priorities on European arms agreements if a united Germany joined NATO.

Gorbachev strongly urged the west not to attempt to impose a European security framework in which a unified Germany would be part of NATO. However, he said that "certain ideas and suggestions" had been put forward for breaking the impasse on a united Germany's military status and that the principal parties would study the matter further.

JUNE
Kohl, in a commencement address at Harvard University, spoke of his vision of a "United States of Europe," open to any who wished to join.

Gorbachev announced for the first time that he could envision west German soldiers remaining in NATO without a parallel role for east German forces in the Warsaw Pact.

JULY
Gorbachev and Kohl announced their agreement that united Germany must become a full member of NATO.

Kohl agreed to limit the troop strength of a united Germany to 370,000 and was expected to give as yet undefined assistance to the USSR to facilitate the removal of the 350,000 Soviet troops in the GDR over the next "three to four years." He added, "NATO structures will not apply" in the east as long as Soviet troops remain there.

AUGUST
Genscher pledged that united Germany would not "manufacture, possess or have control over nuclear, biological and [sic] chemical weapons."

Saddam Hussein invaded Kuwait.

NATO allies unanimously condemned Iraq's actions, but Germany declined a direct role in a military build-up to oppose Hussein.

Germany joined in strict economic sanctions against Iraq.

The "Polish border issue" was reconciled at the 2+4 talks when both Germanies agreed that a united Germany would in "the shortest possible time" complete a treaty guaranteeing Poland's borders.

SEPTEMBER
The Treaty on the Final Settlement with Respect to Germany (2+4 Treaty) was signed on September 12.

The 2+4 agreement reached in Moscow effectively ended Soviet opposition to German unification.

The United States announced withdrawal of 60,000 U.S. troops and the closing of several U.S.-operated installations in Germany over the next few years. Bonn welcomed the announcement.

Italian Foreign Minister Gianni de Michelis announced on September 18 that Italy would present (to EC foreign and prime ministers) in October 1990 a plan to "merge" the WEU and the regular European Political Cooperation (EPC) mechanism for dovetailing the 12 EC states' foreign policies.

Germany agreed to pay DM 12 billion for withdrawal of Soviet troops from its soil.

Obligatory military service in Germany was reduced from 15 to 12 months.

Germany offered DM 3.3 billion in support of the U.S. military effort in the Persian Gulf.

A two-thirds majority of each German parliament ratified terms of the unification treaty to become effective October 3.

OCTOBER
October 3 was German unification day.

On the same day, Baker announced agreement in principle within CSCE on limits on conventional forces in Europe.

The Bundestag voted to approve a treaty between the FRG and the USSR regulating the stationing and withdrawal of 600,000 Soviets from eastern Germany. Part of the treaty ensured German financial support while the troops remained in the east. The total financial cost of the treaty to Germany was estimated by federal government officials to be in the range of DM 13 billion. A December 31, 1994 deadline for Soviet withdrawal was agreed upon.

A 4,200-man German-French brigade was established in Baden-Wurttemberg.

The Federal Labor Agency in Nuremberg announced that unemployment in the eastern part of Germany rose by 83,500 to reach a total of 444,825, a rate of 5 percent, since monetary union. The agency also reported that the number of people working reduced hours totaled 1,771,576 in mid-September.

NOVEMBER
Willy Brandt's mission to Iraq as Chairman of the Socialist International caused anger in Washington and criticism from the Bonn government.

The Bundestag debate on the Persian Gulf revealed Germans were divided on use of force and effectiveness of economic sanctions.

In Bonn, Kohl and Gorbachev signed three treaties. The first was a general treaty of friendship and cooperation; the second dealt with economic cooperation; and the third provided for cooperation between labor and social service agencies.

Cheney announced a significant build-up in U.S. troop strength in the Persian Gulf, a number of whom would proceed there from their normal stations in Germany.

Genscher and Polish Foreign Minister Krzysztof Skubiszewski signed the German-Polish border treaty in Warsaw on November 14.

Bush visited Kohl and discussed the upcoming CSCE conference as well as the crisis in the Gulf.

The CSCE Conference in Paris on November 19-21 finished with the signing of the "Paris Charter for a New Europe: A New Age of Democracy." Among the provisions was the first CSCE organization in Vienna, the Center for Conflict Resolution. A secretariat for the CSCE is to be established in Prague. Troop ceilings for NATO and the Warsaw Pact forces, agreed to in principle in October in preparatory CSCE meetings, were endorsed. The Vienna negotiations on conventional forces were projected to continue until 1992. Increased cooperation on European security matters was called for.

At the same time as the CSCE Paris meeting, a *TransAtlantic Declaration* was signed between the United States and Europe and between Canada and Europe. This document acknowledged the deep transatlantic ties and pledged the signatories to safeguard peace, promote open trade and meet semiannually at the highest levels to consult on common interests. Genscher said that this agreement as well as the CSCE would cement America's role as a "partner in the new European order."

Kohl asked Germans to send food and other aid to the USSR. By the end of November, nearly DM 900 million had been collected.

The FRG interior ministry announced that roughly 25,000 eastern Germans had moved west each month since the July currency union. Before the March 18 elections in the GDR, approximately 10,000 GDR citizens had come west each week.

During the German election campaign, Kohl promised to move toward greater latitude for the Chancellor in using German military forces. Opposition parties argued that such a move would require amendment of the Basic Law based on an absolute two-thirds majority of both legislative houses.

DECEMBER
The first all-German elections in almost 60 years took place on December 2, 1990. The ruling coalition of CDU/CSU and the FDP won enough votes to remain in power. The SPD made a poorer showing than in the 1987 election. The Green Party in the west did not garner enough votes to break the 5 percent barrier. But because of the separate 5 percent barrier in the east and west, the Alliance '90/Green Party from the east will be represented. The Party of Democratic Socialism (SED, the former east German communists) also won representation in the Bundestag.

Although the Social Democrats took only 33.5 percent of the vote, they remained in a position to block amendments to the Basic Law, making it difficult, if not unlikely, that the Chancellor would open the amendment process.

Kohl and Mitterrand put forward proposals on how to foster European political union. Their major proposal was to initiate majority votes on all issues before the European Council. They also proposed strengthening the European Parliament and European cooperation on defense matters.

On December 15, the European Council held a summit to begin discussions on European political union and to continue consultations on European economic and monetary union. At the summit, leaders decided to establish an ongoing Inter-governmental Conference to discuss, among other items, expanding EC scope in matters of foreign and defense policy. A continued role for NATO and closer cooperation between the EC and the WEU were discussed. The Italian plan for merger of the latter two institutions was not endorsed.

German editorial opinion on the Gulf crisis remained mixed. There was general support for the UN resolutions. German military participation in coalition activity remained a topic widely avoided. Deployment of NATO Mobile Force air assets, including German personnel and equipment to Turkey at that nation's request, received cautious support from German commentators.

On December 20, Shevardnadze resigned on the basis that he believed reactionary forces in the Soviet Union had set a course on unseating Gorbachev. Politburo reaction showed clear evidence of dissatisfaction among military leaders with *perestroika*.

Protocol to the North Atlantic Treaty on the Accession of the Federal Republic of Germany

Paris, October 23, 1954

The Parties to the North Atlantic Treaty signed at Washington on April 4, 1949,

Being satisfied that the security of the North Atlantic area will be enhanced by the accession of the Federal Republic of Germany to that Treaty, and

Having noted that the Federal Republic of Germany has, by a declaration dated October 3, 1954, accepted the obligations set forth in Article 2 of the Charter of the United Nations and has undertaken upon its accession to the North Atlantic Treaty to refrain from any action inconsistent with the strictly defensive charter of the Treaty, and

Having further noted that all member governments have associated themselves with the declaration also made on October 3, 1954, by the Governments of the United States of America, the United Kingdom of Great Britain and Northern Ireland and the French Republic in connection with the aforesaid declaration of the Federal Republic of Germany,

Agree as follows:

Article 1

Upon the entry into force of the present Protocol, the Government of the United States of America shall on behalf of all the Parties communicate to the Government of the Federal Republic of Germany an invitation to accede to the North Atlantic Treaty. Thereafter the Federal Republic of Germany shall become a Party to that Treaty of the date when it deposits its instruments of accession with the Government of the United States of America in accordance with Article 10 of the Treaty.

Article 2

The present Protocol shall enter into force, when (a) each of the Parties to the North Atlantic Treaty has notified to the Government of the United States of America its acceptance thereof, (b) all instruments of ratification of the Protocol modifying and completing the Brussels Treaty have been deposited with the Belgian Government, and (c) all instruments of ratification or approval of the Convention on the Presence of Foreign Forces in the Federal Republic of Germany have been deposited with the Government of the Federal Republic of Germany. The Government of the United States of America shall inform the other Parties to the North Atlantic Treaty of the date of the receipt of each notification of the acceptance of the present Protocol and of the date of the entry into force of the present Protocol.

Article 3

The present Protocol, of which the English and French texts are equally authentic, shall be deposited in the Archives of the Government of the United States of America. Duly certified copies thereof shall be transmitted by that Government to the Governments of the other Parties to the North Atlantic Treaty.

Treaty on the Final Settlement with Respect to Germany

The Federal Republic of Germany, the German Democratic Republic, the French Republic, the Union of Soviet Socialist Republics, the United Kingdom of Great Britain and Northern Ireland and the United States of America,

Conscious of the fact that their peoples have been living together in peace since 1945;

Mindful of the recent historic changes in Europe which make it possible to overcome the division of the continent;

Having regard to the rights and responsibilities of the Four Powers relating to Berlin and to Germany as a whole, and the corresponding wartime and post-war agreements and decisions of the Four Powers;

Resolved in accordance with their obligations under the Charter of the United Nations to develop friendly relations among nations based on respect for the principle of equal rights and self determination of peoples, and to take other appropriate measures to strengthen universal peace;

Recalling the principles of the Final Act of the Conference on Security and Cooperation in Europe, signed in Helsinki;

Recognizing that those principles have laid firm foundations for the establishment of a just and lasting peaceful order in Europe;

Determined to take account of everyone's security interests;

Convinced of the need finally to overcome antagonism and to develop cooperation in Europe;

Confirming their readiness to reinforce security, in particular by adopting effective arms control, disarmament and confidence-building measures; their willingness not to regard each other as adversaries but to work for a relationship of trust and cooperation; and accordingly their readiness to consider positively setting up appropriate institutional arrangements within the framework of the Conference on Security and Cooperation in Europe;

Welcoming the fact that the German people, freely exercising their right of self-determination, have expressed their will to bring about the unity of Germany as a state so they will be able to serve the peace of the world as an equal and sovereign partner in a united Europe;

Convinced that the unification of Germany as a state with definitive borders is a significant contribution to peace and stability in Europe;

Intending to conclude the final settlement with respect to Germany;

Recognizing that thereby, and with the unification of Germany as a democratic and peaceful state, the rights and responsibilities of the Four Powers relating to Berlin and to Germany as a whole lose their function;

Represented by their Ministers for Foreign Affairs who, in accordance with the Ottawa Declaration of 13 February 1990, met in Bonn on 5 May 1990, in Berlin on 22 June 1990, in Paris on 17 July 1990 with the participation of the Minister for Foreign Affairs of the Republic of Poland, and in Moscow on 12 September 1990;

Have agreed as follows:

Article 1

(1) The united Germany shall comprise the territory of the Federal Republic of Germany, the German Democratic Republic and the whole of Berlin. Its external borders shall be the borders of the Federal Republic of Germany and the German Democratic Republic and shall be definitive from the date on which the present Treaty comes into force. The confirmation of the definitive nature of the borders of the united Germany is an essential element of the peaceful order in Europe.

(2) The united Germany and the Republic of Poland shall confirm the existing border between them in a treaty that is binding under international law.

(3) The united Germany has no territorial claims whatsoever against other states and shall not assert any in the future.

(4) The Governments of the Federal Republic of Germany and the German Democratic Republic shall insure that the constitution of the united Germany does not contain any provision incompatible with these principles. This applies accordingly to the provisions laid down in the preamble, the second sentence of Article 23, and Article 146 of the Basic Law for the Federal Republic of Germany.

(5) The Governments of the French Republic, the Union of Soviet Socialist Republics, the United Kingdom of Great Britain and Northern Ireland, and the United States of America take formal note of the corresponding commitments and declarations by the Governments of the Federal Republic of Germany and the German Democratic Republic and declare that their implementation will confirm the definitive nature of the united Germany's borders.

Article 2

The Governments of the Federal Republic of Germany and the German Democratic Republic reaffirm their declarations that only peace will emanate from German soil. According to the constitution of the united Germany, acts tending to and undertaken with the intent to disturb the peaceful relations between nations, especially to prepare for aggressive war, are unconstitutional and a punishable offense. The Governments of the Federal Republic of Germany and the German Democratic Republic declare that the united Germany will never employ any of its weapons except in accordance with its constitution and the Charter of the United Nations.

Article 3
(1) The Governments of the Federal Republic of Germany and the German Democratic Republic reaffirm their renunciation of the manufacture and possession of and control over nuclear, biological and chemical weapons. They declare that the united Germany, too, will abide by these commitments. In particular, rights and obligations arising from the Treaty on the Non-Proliferation of Nuclear Weapons of July 1, 1968 will continue to apply to the united Germany.

(2) The Government of the Federal Republic of Germany, acting in full agreement with the Government of the German Democratic Republic, made the following statement on 30 August 1990 in Vienna at the Negotiations on Conventional Armed Forces in Europe:
"The Government of the Federal Republic of Germany undertakes to reduce the personnel strength of the armed forces of the united Germany to 370,000 (ground, air and naval forces) within three to four years. This reduction will commence on the entry into force of the first CFE agreement. Within the scope of this overall ceiling no more than 345,000 will belong to the ground and air forces which, pursuant to the agreed mandate, along are the subject of the Negotiations on Conventional Armed Forces in Europe. It assumes that in follow-on negotiations the other participants in the negotiations, too, will render their contribution to enhancing security and stability in Europe, including measures to limit personnel strengths."
The Government of the German Democratic Republic has expressly associated itself with this statement.

(3) The Governments of the French Republic, the Union of Soviet Socialist Republics, the United Kingdom of Great Britain and Northern Ireland, and the United States of America take note of these statements by the Governments of the Federal Republic of Germany and the German Democratic Republic.

Article 4
(1) The Governments of the Federal Republic of Germany, the German Democratic Republic and the Union of Soviet Socialist Republics will settle by treaty the conditions for and the duration of the presence of Soviet armed forces on the territory of the present German Democratic Republic and of Berlin, as well as the conduct of the withdrawal of these armed forces which will be completed by the end of 1994, in connection with the implementation of the undertaking of the Federal Republic of Germany and the German Democratic Republic referred to in paragraph 2 of Article 3 of the present Treaty.

(2) The Governments of the French Republic, the United Kingdom of Great Britain and Northern Ireland and the United States of America take note of this statement.

Article 5
(1) Until the completion of the withdrawal of the Soviet armed forces from the territory of the present German Democratic Republic and of

Berlin in accordance with Article 4 of the present Treaty, only German territorial defense units which are not integrated into the alliance structures to which German armed forces in the rest of German territory are assigned will be stationed in that territory as armed forces of the united Germany. During that period and subject to the provisions of paragraph 2 of this Article, armed forces of other states will not be stationed in that territory or carry out any other military activity there.

(2) For the duration of the presence of Soviet armed forces in the territory of the present German Democratic Republic and of Berlin, armed forces of the French Republic, the United Kingdom of Great Britain and Northern Ireland and the United States of America will, upon German request, remain stationed in Berlin by agreement to this effect between the Government of the united Germany and the Governments of the states concerned. The number of troops and the amount of equipment of all non-German armed forces stationed in Berlin will not be greater than at the time of signature of the present Treaty. New categories of weapons will not be introduced there by non-German armed forces. The Government of the united Germany will conclude with the Governments of those states which have armed forces stationed in Berlin treaties with conditions which are fair taking account of the relations existing with the states concerned.

(3) Following the completion of the withdrawal of the Soviet armed forces from the territory of the present German Democratic Republic and of Berlin, units of German armed forces assigned to military alliance structures in the same way as those in the rest of German territory may also be stationed in that part of Germany, but without nuclear weapon carriers. This does not apply to conventional weapons systems which may have other capabilities in addition to conventional ones but which in that part of Germany are equipped for a conventional role and designated only for such. Foreign armed forces and nuclear weapons or their carriers will not be stationed in that part of Germany or deployed there.

Article 6
The right of the united Germany to belong to alliances, with all the rights and responsibilities rising therefrom, shall not be affected by the present Treaty.

Article 7
(1) The French Republic, the Union of Soviet Socialist Republics, the United Kingdom of Great Britain and Northern Ireland, and the United States of American hereby terminate their rights and responsibilities relating to Berlin and to Germany as a whole. As a result, the corresponding, related quadripartite agreements, decisions and practices are terminated and all related Four Power institutions are dissolved.

(2) The united Germany shall have accordingly full sovereignty over its internal and external affairs.

Article 8
(1) The present Treaty is subject to ratification or acceptance as soon as possible. On the German side it will be ratified by the united Germany. The Treaty will therefore apply to the united Germany.

(2) The instruments of ratification or acceptance shall be deposited with the Government of the united Germany. That Government shall inform the Governments of the other Contracting Parties of the deposit of each instrument of ratification of acceptance.

Article 9
The present Treaty shall enter into force for the united Germany, the French Republic, the Union of Soviet Socialist Republics, the United Kingdom of Great Britain and Northern Ireland, and the United States of America on the date of deposit of the last instrument of ratification or acceptance by these states.

Article 10
The original of the present Treaty, of which the English, French, German and Russian texts are equally authentic, shall be deposited with the Government of the Federal Republic of Germany, which shall transmit certified true copies to the Governments of the other Contracting Parties.

Declaration Between
the European Community
and the United States

Transatlantic Declaration Between the European Community and the United States agreed upon during the summit meeting of the Conference on Security and Cooperation in Europe (CSCE)

November 19-21, 1990 in Paris

The United States of America on one side and, on the other, the European Community and its member states,
–mindful of their common heritage and of their close historical, political, economic and cultural ties,
–guided by their faith in the values of human dignity, intellectual freedom and civil liberties, and in the democratic institutions which have evolved on both sides of the Atlantic over the centuries,
–recognizing that the transatlantic solidarity has been essential for the preservation of peace and freedom and for the development of free and prosperous economies as well as for the recent developments which have restored unity in Europe,
–determined to help consolidate the new Europe, undivided and democratic,
–resolved to strengthen security, economic cooperation and human rights in Europe in the framework of the CSCE, and in other fora,
–noting the firm commitment of the United States and the EC member states concerned to the North Atlantic Alliance and to its principles and purposes,
–acting on the basis of a pattern of cooperation proven over many decades, and convinced that by strengthening and expanding this partnership on an equal footing they will greatly contribute to continued stability, as well as to political and economic progress in Europe and in the world,
–aware of their shared responsibility, not only to further common interests but also to face transnational challenges affecting the well-being of all mankind,
–bearing in mind the accelerating process by which the European Community is acquiring its own identity in economic and monetary matters, in foreign policy and in the domain of security,
–determined further to strengthen transatlantic solidarity, through the variety of their international relations,
have decided to endow their relationship with long-term perspectives.

Common Goals
The United States of America and the European Community and its member states solemnly reaffirm their determination further to

strengthen their partnership in order to:
–support democracy, the rule of law and respect for human rights and individual liberty, and promote prosperity and social progress worldwide;
–safeguard peace and promote international security, by cooperating with other nations against aggression and coercion, by contributing to the settlement of conflicts in the world and by reinforcing the role of the United Nations and other international organizations;
–pursue policies aimed at achieving a sound world economy marked by sustained economic growth with low inflation, a high level of employment, equitable social conditions, in a framework of international stability;
–promote market principles, reject protectionism and expand, strengthen and further open the multilateral trading system;
–carry out their resolve to help developing countries by all appropriate means in their efforts towards political and economic reforms;
–provide adequate support, in cooperation with other states and organizations, to the nations of eastern and central Europe undertaking economic and political reforms and encourage their participation in the multilateral institutions of international trade and finance.

Principles of US-EC Partnership
To achieve their common goals, the European Community and its member states and the United States of America will inform and consult each other on important matters of common interest, both political and economic, with a view to bringing their positions as independents. In appropriate international bodies, in particular, they will seek close cooperation.

The EC-US partnership will, moreover, greatly benefit from the mutual knowledge and understanding acquired through regular consultations as described in this declaration.

Economic Cooperation
Both sides recognize the importance of strengthening the multilateral trading system. They will support further steps towards liberalization, transparency, and the implementation of GATT and OECD principles concerning both trade in goods and services and investment.

They will further develop their dialogue, which is already underway, on other matters such as technical and non-tariff barriers to industrial and agricultural trade, services, competition policy, transportation policy standards, telecommunications, high technology and other relevant areas.

Education, Scientific, and Cultural Cooperation
The partnership between the European Community and its member states on the one hand, and the United States on the other, will be based on continuous efforts to strengthen mutual cooperation in various other fields which directly affect the present and future well-being

of their citizens, such as exchanges and joint projects in science and technology, including, inter alia, research in medicine, environment protection, pollution prevention, energy, space, high-energy physics, and the safety of nuclear and other installations, as well as in education and culture, including academic and youth exchanges.

Trans-national Challenges
The United States of America and the European Community and its member states will fulfill their responsibility to address trans-national challenges, in the interest of their own peoples and of the rest of the world. In particular, they will join their efforts in the following fields:
–combatting and preventing terrorism;
–putting an end to the illegal production, trafficking and consumption of narcotics and related criminal activities, such as the laundering of money;
–cooperating in the fight against international crime;
–protecting the environment, both internationally and domestically, by integrating environmental and economic goals;
–preventing the proliferation of nuclear armaments, chemical and biological weapons, and missile technology.

Institutional Framework for Consultation
Both sides agree that a framework is required for regular and intensive consultation. They will make full use of and further strengthen existing procedures, including those established by the president of the European Council and the president of the United States on 27th February 1990, namely:
–Bi-annual consultations to be arranged in the United States and in Europe between, on the one side, the president of the European Council and the president of the commission, and on the other side, the president of the United States;
–Bi-annual consultations between the European Community foreign ministers, with the commission, and the U.S. secretary of state, alternately on either side of the Atlantic;
–Ad hoc consultations between the presidency, foreign minister or the troika and the U.S. secretary of state;
—Bi-annual consultations between the commission and the U.S. government at the cabinet level;
–Briefings, as currently exist, by the presidency to U.S. representatives on the European Political Cooperation (EPC) meeting at the ministerial level.

Both sides are resolved to develop and deepen these procedures for consultation so as to reflect the evolution of the European Community and of its relationship with the United States.

They welcome the actions taken by the European Parliament and the Congress of the United States in order to improve their dialogue and thereby bring closer together the peoples on both sides of the Atlantic.

Index

National Planning Association

NPA is an independent, private, nonprofit, nonpolitical organization that carries on research and policy formulation in the public interest. NPA was founded during the Great Depression of the 1930s when conflicts among the major economic groups—business, labor, agriculture—threatened to paralyze national decisionmaking on the critical issues confronting American society. It was dedicated to the task of getting these diverse groups to work together to narrow areas of controversy and broaden areas of agreement as well as to map out specific programs for action in the best traditions of a functioning democracy. Such democratic and decentralized planning, NPA believes, involves the development of effective governmental and private policies and programs not only by official agencies but also through the independent initiative and cooperation of the main private sector groups concerned.

To this end, NPA brings together influential and knowledgeable leaders from business, labor, agriculture, and the applied and academic professions to serve on policy committees. These committees identify emerging problems confronting the nation at home and abroad and seek to develop and agree upon policies and programs for coping with them. The research and writing for these committees are provided by NPA's professional staff and, as required, by outside experts.

In addition, NPA's professional staff undertakes research through its central or "core" program designed to provide data and ideas for policymakers and planners in government and the private sector. These activities include research on national goals and priorities, productivity and economic growth, welfare and dependency problems, employment and human resource needs, and technological change; analyses and forecasts of changing international realities and their implications for U.S. policies; and analyses of important new economic, social and political realities confronting American society.

In developing its staff capabilities, NPA has increasingly emphasized two related qualifications. First is the interdisciplinary knowledge required to understand the complex nature of many real-life problems. Second is the ability to bridge the gap between theoretical or highly technical research and the practical needs of policymakers and planners in government and the private sector.

Through its committees and its core program, NPA addresses a wide range of issues. Not all of the NPA Trustees or committee members are in full agreement with all that is contained in these publications unless such endorsement is specifically stated.

NPA Committee on Changing International Realities

The Committee on Changing International Realities was established by the National Planning Association in 1975 to improve understanding of the challenges confronting the U.S. private and public sectors in the international economy. In accordance with NPA's practice, the CIR is composed of leaders from industry, finance, agriculture, labor, and the academic and applied professions. By bringing together key representatives from such diverse concerns and perspectives, the Committee is uniquely qualified to aid in the formulation of effective economic and foreign policies.

The CIR undertakes a continuing program with three primary purposes: (1) to give private sector leaders the opportunity to discuss in an informal atmosphere, and with public policymakers, the challenges and problems facing them in the international economy; (2) to interpret the changes in the international environment that may affect U.S. private sector interests or provide new opportunities; and (3) to encourage the formulation of better public policies by sponsoring nonpartisan research studies on the factors affecting U.S. competitiveness and international economic interests.

In recent years, the CIR has focused on the challenges to U.S. competitiveness posed by Japan and the newly industrializing countries; European plans to form an internal market by 1992; the growth of regional trading blocs; the tensions between global corporations and nation-states; changing U.S. relations with and interests in Mexico and other developing countries; strains in the international financial system; and the consequences of macroeconomic policies for U.S. trade performance.

The Committee meets twice a year to discuss, together with experts in the field, pressing national and international issues. At these meetings it also focuses on subjects to be researched, reviews outlines and drafts of studies under way and considers their policy implications. Detailed guidance of the CIR's research program is carried on by subcommittees.

For further information about the CIR's continuing activities, please contact:

Richard S. Belous
NPA Vice President, International Affairs,
and CIR Director

National Planning Association
1424 16th Street, N.W., Suite 700
Washington, D.C. 20036
(202) 265-7685
Fax (202) 797-5516

Members of the Committee on Changing International Realities

JOHN J. SIMONE
Chair;
Group Executive,
Manufacturers Hanover
Trust Company

EDWARD J. CARLOUGH
Vice Chair;
General President, Sheet Metal
Workers' International Association

C. MICHAEL AHO
Director of Economic Studies and
the International Trade Project,
Council on Foreign Relations, Inc.

J. ROBERT ANDERSON
Vice Chairman,
Bridgestone/Firestone, Inc.

ALBERT D. ANGEL
Vice President for Public Affairs,
Merck & Co., Inc.

HANS W. BECHERER
Chairman and
Chief Executive Officer,
Deere and Company

GEORGE BECKER
International Vice President
(Administration),
United Steelworkers of America

WILLIAM H. BYWATER
International President,
International Union of
Electronic, Electrical,
Salaried, Machine and
Furniture Workers, AFL-CIO

JOE E. CHENOWETH
Senior Corporate Vice President,
International,
Honeywell, Inc.

J.G. CLARKE
Director and
Senior Vice President,
Exxon Corporation

DOMINIQUE CLAVEL
Senior Vice President,
Chase Manhattan Bank, N.A.

RICHARD N. COOPER
Maurits C. Boas Professor
of International Economics,
Center for International Affairs,
Harvard University

RICHARD V.L. COOPER
Ernst & Young

KENNETH W. DAM
Vice President,
Law & External Relations,
IBM Corporation

THIBAUT de SAINT PHALLE
Saint Phalle International Group

LODEWIJK deVINK
Executive Vice President
and President,
U.S. Operations,
Warner-Lambert Company

BARBARA J. EASTERLING
Executive Vice President,
Communications Workers of
America

MURRAY H. FINLEY
President Emeritus,
Amalgamated Clothing &
Textile Workers' Union;
Chairman of the Advisory
Committee, Amalgamated Bank
of New York

THEODORE GEIGER
Distinguished Research Professor
of Intersocietal Relations,
School of Foreign Service,
Georgetown University

MELVYN GOETZ
Director of Corporate
Development,
Westinghouse Electric Corporation

175

RALPH W. GOLBY
New York, New York

LAURENCE W. HECHT
Executive Director,
Iacocca Institute,
Lehigh University

ROLF HENEL
President,
Lederle International,
American Cyanamid Company

ROBERT HERZSTEIN
Partner,
Shearman and Sterling

JOHN H. JACKSON
Professor of Law,
University of Michigan Law School

ROBERT F. KELLEY
Managing Partner,
Governmental Affairs,
Arthur Andersen & Co.

KORETSUGU KODAMA
Chairman,
Bank of Tokyo, Ltd.

RICHARD J. KOGAN
President and
Chief Operating Officer,
Schering-Plough Corporation

MYRON R. LASERSON
Huntington, New York

ARTHUR M. LERNER
Vice President,
Corporate Development,
Siemens Corporation

ARTHUR R. LOEVY
Secretary-Treasurer,
Amalgamated Clothing & Textile
Workers' Union

ROLAND E. MAGNIN
Executive Vice President,
Xerox Corporation

JOHN R. MALLOY
Senior Vice President of
External Affairs,
E.I. Dupont de Nemours & Co.

DONALD E. MARQUART
Executive Vice President,
International Sector,
Square D Company

EDWARD E. MASTERS
President,
National Planning Association

HON. CHARLES McC. MATHIAS, JR.
Partner,
Jones, Day, Reavis & Pogue

HENRY McINTYRE
Founder of the Population
Resource Center

JOHN MILLER
Chocorua, New Hampshire

LINDA NEELY
Vice President,
Human Resources,
British Aerospace

S.F. O'MALLEY
Chairman and Senior Partner,
Price Waterhouse

RUDOLPH A. OSWALD
Director,
Department of Economic Research,
AFL-CIO

MYER RASHISH
President,
Rashish Associates, Inc.

ROBERT REISER
Senior Lecturer,
Management Department,
Babson College

DAVIS R. ROBINSON
Partner,
LeBoeuf, Lamb, Leiby & MacRae

HERBERT SALZMAN
Bradford Associates

HOWARD D. SAMUEL
President,
Industrial Union Department,
AFL-CIO

NATHANIEL SAMUELS
Advisory Director,
Shearson Lehman Hutton Inc.

PHILIP D. SHERMAN
Senior Vice President,
Investment Bank Sector,
Citicorp, N.A.

WINFRIED H. SPAEH
Executive Vice President
and Senior General Manager,
Dresdner Bank AG

HANS G. STORR
Senior Vice President and
Chief Financial Officer,
Philip Morris Companies, Inc.

HARRY W. STRACHAN
Director,
Bain & Company

STEPHEN VEHSLAGE
Assistant General Manager
of U.S. Education,
IBM United States

JOHN T. WATSON
Administrative Director,
International Operations,
Pioneer Hi-Bred International, Inc.

ROBERT A. WILSON
Vice President-Public Affairs,
Pfizer, Inc.

ALAN WM. WOLFF
Dewey, Ballantine, Bushby,
Palmer & Wood

CHARLES G. WOOTTON
Coordinator,
International Public Affairs,
Chevron Corporation

RALPH S. YOHE
Mt. Horeb, Wisconsin

EUGENE W. ZELTMANN
Manager of Trade and Industry
Associations,
GE Industry and
Power Systems Sales,
General Electric Company

NPA Publications

United Germany and the United States, by Michael A. Freney and Rebecca S. Hartley (196 pp, 1991, $17.50), CIR #21.

Taking Advantage of America's Window of Opportunity, A Statement by the Board of Trustees of the National Planning Association (16 pp, 1990, $2.50), NPA #248.

Creating a Strong Post-Cold War Economy, by Richard S. Belous (40 pp, 1990, $8.00), NPA #247.

Preparing for Change: Workforce Excellence in a Turbulent Economy, Recommendations of the Committee on New American Realities (32 pp, 1990, $5.00), NAR #5.

Changing Sources of U.S. Economic Growth, 1950-2010: A Chartbook of Trends and Projections, by Nestor E. Terleckyj (76 pp, 1990, $15.00), NPA #244.

The Growth of Regional Trading Blocs in the Global Economy, ed. Richard S. Belous and Rebecca S. Hartley (168 pp, 1990, $15.00), NPA #243.

Dealing with the Budget Deficit, by Rudolph G. Penner (52 pp, 1989, $5.00), NAR #4.

On Preserving Shared Values, A British-North American Committee Statement on the 40th Anniversary of the Signing of the North Atlantic Treaty (16 pp, 1989, $2.00), BN #37.

The Contingent Economy: The Growth of the Temporary, Part-Time and Subcontracted Workforce, by Richard S. Belous (136 pp, 1989, $15.00), NPA #239.

Positioning Agriculture for the 1990s: A New Decade of Change, Symposium Papers sponsored by the Agribusiness Council of the Chamber of Commerce of Greater Kansas City and the Food and Agriculture Committee of the National Planning Association (160 pp, 1989, $12.00), FAC #7.

The 1992 Challenge from Europe: Development of the European Community's Internal Market, by Michael Calingaert (176 pp, 1988, with 1990 Foreword by the author, $15.00), NPA #236.

The GATT Negotiations 1986-1990: Origins, Issues and Prospects, by Sidney Golt (120 pp, 1988, $10.00), BN #36.

NPA membership is $65.00 per year, tax deductible. In addition to new NPA publications, members receive *Looking Ahead,* a quarterly journal, which is also available at the separate subscription price of $35.00. NPA members, upon request, may obtain a 30 percent discount on other publications in stock. A list of publications will be provided upon request. Quantity discounts are given.

Canada-U.S. Outlook, published quarterly by NPA, is available through a separate subscription rate of $35.00 per year.

NPA is a qualified nonprofit, charitable organization under section 501(c)(3) of the Internal Revenue Code.

NATIONAL PLANNING ASSOCIATION
1424 16th Street, N.W., Suite 700
Washington, D.C. 20036
Tel (202)265-7685 Fax (202)797-5516